A CENTURY OF
REMEMBRANCE

Published by IWM, Lambeth Road, London SE1 6HZ
iwm.org.uk

ISBN 978-1-912423-02-6

A catalogue record for this book is
available from the British Library.
Printed and bound in Italy by Printer Trento
Colour reproduction by DL Imaging

Every effort has been made to contact all copyright
holders. The publishers will be glad to make good
in future editions any error or omissions brought
to their attention.

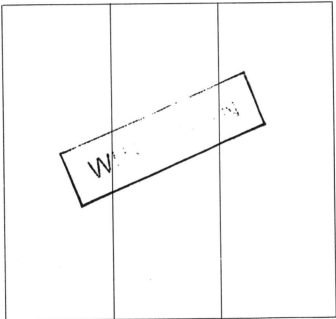

A CENTURY OF

REMEMBRANCE

Laura Clouting

IWM
IMPERIAL WAR MUSEUMS

CONTENTS

THE "CEASE FIRE."
November 11th, 1918.
(facsimile.)

O.C. A Corps. *[initials]*   URGENT
      B
      C
      D
OC no 3 Sect. M.G.C. (Malta Artists)

          Hostilities will cease at
11 a.m. to day.
          Form up and march
back independently to the
Château, HARVENG at once
Do not forget to bring the
cookers with you.

                              G. Paterson
09.30 hrs   Lt & Adj.
11.11.18.

INTRODUCTION

Each November, British people are called upon 'to remember'. These cries have consistently roused a significant swathe of the population to action, one hundred years after they were first heard. It was the 'Great War', which saw so many lives wiped out in pursuit of victory, that embedded remembrance in the national consciousness — as a concept, as a duty, as an emotion — and that gave it expression in art and architecture, through observance at emotive events and even through its own vocabulary.

Respect. Reverence. Remembrance. The lexicon of the annual commemoration is so familiar. Yet surprisingly, given its prevalence, the term 'remembrance' itself remains nebulous. Even its subject is disputed. The focus is traditionally upon those who have given their lives while serving in Britain and its Empire or Commonwealth's armed forces or associated voluntary organisations. But increasingly it is argued that the rituals associated with remembrance every November should be more firmly inclusive of all who have died as a result of war, both civilian and military.

In its most recognisable forms remembrance is channelled through a profusion of red poppies, services at stone memorials and the contemplative observance of a two minute silence. Over the past century these solemnities have acted as the cornerstones of the nation's act of collective mourning. The annual commemorations have proved tenaciously resistant to change. At times they have served as a lightning rod for challenge by those who decry perceived hypocrisy or collective mawkishness when it comes to paying tribute to the British war dead. The very familiarity of the commemorations arguably also risks inertia. Do we understand what we are meant to be remembering?

Whatever the motivation, consideration of those who have fought and died serving in Britain's armed forces feels like a duty few of us wish to dispense with. This is perhaps all the more remarkable because, increasingly, most who heed the calls to remember have no first-hand experience of conflict nor any surviving direct connection to the experience of war. For so many, remembrance means a reflection on the tragic loss of mostly young lives in pursuit of earnest, well-meaning and self-sacrificing causes. It can take the form of an appreciative recognition of those who have died in conflicts to protect national interests. It is perhaps a moment of agreement that Britain may not have enjoyed years of relative stability without the efforts of servicemen and women in the wars of the past century — wars that came at an immense human cost.

For more recent conflicts, where consensus has been more difficult to achieve, remembrance has shifted from a sense of collective mass loss following the world wars to a tighter focus on individual lives — where single fatalities became leading news stories in their own right while conflicts were ongoing. Remembrance is increasingly heightened by a sense that many of us would never

---

Opposite: Notice of the 'cease fire' as issued to the Artists Rifles regiment on 11 November 1918. The news spread through formal channels down to front line soldiers; it had been preceded by rumours in the days leading up to the Armistice that the war might be almost over.

The Commanding Officer of the 9th Battalion East Surrey Regiment leads a cheer to the king in France the day after the Armistice was signed.

choose to put ourselves in the line of fire or feel able to take another human life in combat. Gone is the idea of 'joining up' en masse to defend the nation in a time of grave emergency, as felt so keenly during the world wars.

Whatever our own participation, whatever our motivations to join in or not, it is clear that the roots of remembrance as we know it lie in the First World War. This seismic conflict and the commemorations that emerged from it are the focus of this book. The war was a long drawn-out, appallingly costly struggle. From its beginnings in August 1914 to the end of the fighting on 11 November 1918, four years of violence ravaged the globe with so-called 'civilised' Europe at its epicentre. It is not possible to understand how remembrance of the war took shape in Britain without appreciating the scale and character of what had quickly become known to contemporaries as the 'Great War'. The conflict's

magnitude was self-evident from this swiftly adopted title. Only with the coming of the Second World War some 20 years later did it acquire the title of the 'First World War'.

The fighting transformed political systems, shattered entire empires and irreversibly altered societal norms. This was war on an unprecedented scale. Economies, industries and technologies were turned over to producing weapons and armaments. Vast quantities of shells and guns poured out of factories, creating a direct bond between workers and the serving soldiers, airmen and sailors who awaited their supplies. Transport played a key role too, as railways and ships raced essential equipment to the front line.

Propagandist appeals to hearts and minds squeezed vital consent from British people so the conflict could continue. The war was perceived as a struggle for national survival. Newspapers, literature and posters carried calls

A jubilant crowd cheers outside Buckingham Palace on Armistice Day. The king and queen appeared on the balcony to acknowledge the hordes of people celebrating outside the palace.

to duty in defence of families, homes, countries and even civilisation itself from a German enemy widely perceived as cruel and barbaric. Personal freedoms were restricted in a way unthinkable prior to the war to maximise resources and to turn Britain into a fortress. Those deemed to be 'enemy aliens' were sent to internment camps. The war hit home in the pocket, too, as the rate of income tax flew skywards to pay for the conflict.

Merciless modern weaponry caused devastating injuries on an unprecedented scale. Innovations in aviation and medicine were drastically accelerated. Bloody battles assumed an epic quality, even to their participants. They took place in wide open skies, on turbulent seas and across swathes of varied terrain, from waterlogged trenches to scorching deserts and snow-capped mountains. Although its origins were rooted in the tensions between the great European powers of the

early twentieth century, and the battles that determined ultimate victory were fought on the continent, this was a truly global conflict. The key belligerents were imperial nations who controlled vast territories. As such, the war drew in diverse forces from far-flung reaches of the world.

For those who lived through it, the First World War was a searing, unforgettable experience. Anxiety, physical discomfort, tedium and chronic stress became a way of life. Sometimes acute, sometimes blunted and dreary, the experience of the conflict saturated people's minds and emotions. Yet it also gave purpose. It afforded comradeship and humour.

After four relentless years, the violence finally stopped. With ceasefires agreed on other fighting fronts, the war's ultimate conclusion occurred on the battlefields of the Western Front. Although rumours of an Armistice there had been spreading at the turn of November 1918,

confirmation was not received until the morning of 11 November. Then the news rapidly spread – all hostilities would cease at 11.00am. Though greeted with widespread relief, many soldiers were too emotionally and physically exhausted to absorb the fact that the fighting had ended. It took time to accept that there was no longer any requirement to kill or risk being killed. By contrast, the celebrations on British streets were rapturous.

The time and date of the Armistice's imposition went on to have immense resonance in Britain. The community and regimental war memorials dotted all over the country were almost always unveiled on the anniversary of the Western Front ceasefire. The date 11 November swiftly established itself in popular consciousness as the focal point of remembrance, inextricably linked to the formalities that followed – including a collective two minute silence at 11am. This date, rather than 4 August, the date that war broke out, seemed more appropriate as a moment to reflect upon the war's calamitous toll.

With eventual peace, thoughts turned to the future. After so much upheaval, destruction and flux, what new world would emerge? Veterans of the fighting fronts and the civilian home fronts became witnesses to a complex transition as a state of 'total war' was wound up. Much energy was spent striving to move forwards, yet the need to make sense of the violence and its human cost became equally consuming. During the war itself, the mounting death toll was a motivating force: only victory could ensure that lives had not been lost in vain. But the spectrum of reactions to the war's ending, from merriment to numbness, reflected the array of attitudes that started to emerge over how to remember – or even whether to forget – the war's fatalities in the long term. A tension developed between a desire to move on and a determination that the lives lost would never fade from people's minds.

Remembrance of the war dead won out. It manifested itself in many spheres: within families, in wider communities and in forms determined by the state. There is no definitive inventory of ways in which the British First World War dead were honoured; these are surprisingly varied and continue to evolve. This book explores many of them. Remembrance encompasses memories, rituals, monuments, objects, events, landscapes and institutions. It was expressed in flowers, murals, stained-glass windows, music and in veteran reunions. Cultural outpourings further influenced perceptions of the war, acting as a conduit for remembrance. Films, books, poems, plays and art developed an informal memorialising function. They combined to offer a uniquely British view of the First World War: that it was chiefly a futile slaughter.

As established and consensual as the most familiar aspects of remembrance seem now, aspirations conflicted at times. Debates were plentiful as commemoration of the lives lost became a fiercely emotive issue. It was certainly not inevitable that the British and Empire war dead, from the First World War onwards, would be remembered in such an expansive manner as they have been. Commemoration of previous wars had focused on military actions or statues of feted leaders, such as Nelson and Wellington. And for many nations the First World War, however terrible, became a muted memory compared to the bloodletting that ravaged the globe between 1939 and 1945.

For Britain, however, the loss of life within its military and volunteer forces during the First World War remains unsurpassed to this day. The methods of commemoration established in the aftermath of the conflict became so firmly entrenched that remembrance of every subsequent conflict's toll has harnessed the formal rituals inherited from the First World War.

The chapters that follow explore the human cost of the 'Great War' for Britain and its Empire, and show the practical and psychological problems posed by mass death on the battlefield. These difficulties crucially influenced the distinctive ways in which remembrance took hold in Britain during the years that followed. Although all belligerent countries found ways to remember their war dead, this book is concerned with the British manifestations – in the home, within communities, on behalf of the nation and through popular culture. The 'war to end all wars' may have failed to prevent the further loss of British lives on the battlefield. Yet it did mark the beginning of a remarkably steadfast commitment to remembrance of the ongoing human cost. Whether public or private, controversial or consensual, the ways we remember reveal as much about ourselves as those we are remembering.

Opposite: A crowd gathers around the newly unveiled Cenotaph in July 1919. The overwhelming public reaction to this memorial, initially intended to be temporary and made of wood, resulted in a permanent stone structure being unveiled one year later. The Cenotaph was to become the primary and permanent focus of remembrance services in Britain.

1

THE 'GREAT WAR'

W hen war was declared in 1914, each side believed in its ability to execute a swift, victorious campaign. Few foresaw the protracted bloodshed that came to define the conflict long after it was concluded. Yet the fighting spectacularly failed to be 'over by Christmas'. The prospect of triumphant peace fuelled energies, efforts and hope on both sides for years – eventually coming to pass for Britain and its allies in 1918.

The defining characteristic of the war was the grievous extent of its casualties. The sum total of the wounds and deaths inflicted is almost always referred to as a 'cost' or a 'toll' – the extinguishing of life on a mass scale. The numbers killed within the forces of many nations were similarly staggering, but the perception of the First World War as something uniquely devastating was a very British view, in part the result of how it recruited its army: civilian volunteers left their communities to fight and sometimes die alongside one another. The loss of life between 1914 and 1918 was tragically superseded for other nations by later turmoil, most especially the Second World War's atrocious military and civilian death count.

Above: Soldiers load a shell into a 15-inch howitzer on the Western Front. The heavy guns that caused so much devastation required many men to load shells, fire and maintain the gun's function in order to pound enemy positions.

Previous page: An infantry unit prepare to leave their trenches for an evening raid on enemy positions during the Macedonia campaign in 1916.

But for Britain, the impact of the First World War's trauma has never been surpassed. The years 1914 to 1918 saw its worst loss of life in a war. Three-quarters of a million servicemen died as a result of the conflict. When combined with the deaths from Britain's Empire forces, the death toll grew nearer to one million lives. The death count also included thousands of women who were killed while volunteering, often as nurses or for female branches of the armed services. Although the death toll once again ran into the hundreds of thousands, British losses in the Second World War were considerably fewer. One quarter of a million servicemen died in that war. Civilian casualties were far greater, though, with some 60,000 people killed in German air raids in Britain. The First World War's human impact extended to the wounded and those who became mentally ill as a result of their war service. The effects on their bodies and psyches were sometimes severe and permanent, never allowing the experience of war to be forgotten. Even those who returned home apparently unscathed were survivors of a seismic event.

After a brief period of fast-moving fighting in 1914, the war stagnated on the Western Front. Heavy guns were deployed in great numbers, unleashing

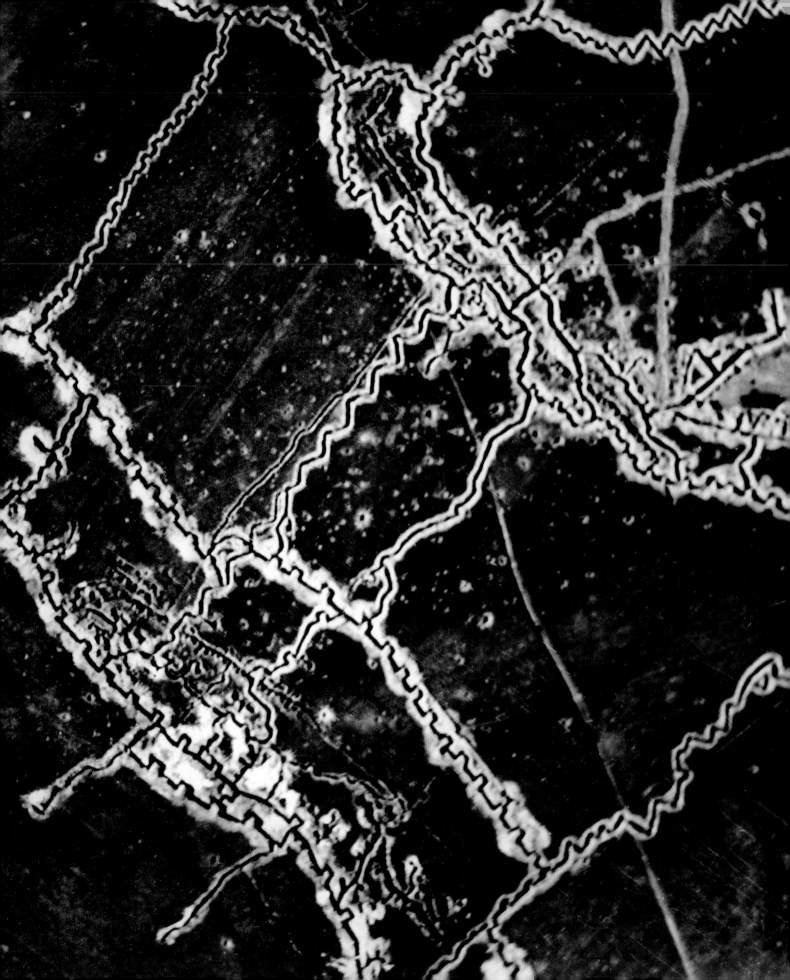

immense destructive firepower; the majority of the war's deaths were inflicted by artillery. Heavy guns made the likelihood of being physically obliterated, mutilated or buried alive by high explosive shells a very real prospect during bombardments. Improved machine guns wreaked their own havoc in combat; their bullets tore through flesh and bone.

TRENCH WARFARE

Trenches were a defensive response to these weapons, as it was simply too dangerous to stand in the open. As the war progressed, fledgling ditches turned into a network of deep and sophisticated hiding places on the Western Front – a 250-mile stretch of trenches that ran from Switzerland to the English Channel, cutting through sand dunes, fields, woods and villages. Though not a new concept in war, trench systems had never been employed on such a scale before. Attempts to break the deadlock were launched on far-flung fronts. Each failed. Yet the Western Front, in stalemate for so long, was where the war's outcome was ultimately decided.

Battle, maintenance and repair set the rhythm of trench life. Hard labour was the only way to make good the damage wrought by enemy shelling. The elements posed even greater travails, as Captain John Cohen advised a friend:

> This horrible country is made of mud, water and dead Germans. Whenever water is left in a trench it drags the earth down on either side and forms a fearful sticky viscous matter that lets you sink gently down and grips you like a vice when you're there. The chief business is riveting and draining, and improving parapets and traverses.

The strip of terrain in between the trenches of opposing forces, known as 'no man's land', was fraught with deadly menace. Sergeant Alexander Mudie, who was killed in action in 1915, wrote regularly to his brother and described its dangers. He explained that 'at certain points there is only a small flat field separating one trench from another and it is almost certain death to show a head above the top of the trench'.

The impossibility of achieving dramatic progress was starkly illustrated by the debris of battle that accumulated over years of to and fro battles over scraps of land. The haunting assortment was described by Major Philip Pilditch in his diary entry on 10 October 1918; just one month before the Armistice:

> On the way back we spent some time in the old No Man's Land of four years' duration, round about Fauquissart and Aubers. It was a morbid but intensely interesting occupation tracing the various battles among

Opposite: An aerial reconnaissance photograph of German positions before the Battle of the Somme in 1916, clearly showing a warren of chalky earth trenches. The trench network on the Western Front was extensively photographed from the air to obtain vital intelligence about enemy activity and positions.

the hundreds of skulls, bones and remains scattered thickly about. The progress of our successive attacks could be clearly seen from the types of equipment on the skeletons, soft caps denoting the 1914 and early 1915 attacks, then respirators, then steel helmets marking attacks in 1916. Also Australian slouch hats, used in the costly and abortive attack in 1916. There were many of those poor remains all along the German wire.

Right: Canadian soldiers make the most of a quieter time during daylight hours to catch up on sleep and write letters home. The night was a busy period for wiring parties, fatigue parties and raiding parties who undertook their work under cover of darkness.

THE EMPIRE AT WAR

The slouch hats noted by Major Pilditch were a symbol of the conflict's scale, reflected in the forces that came to fight for their respective empires. Britain's territories provided vital resources and essential manpower. Thousands of men of different races and religions joined its forces, travelling from Britain's colonies and its self-governing Dominions – Australia, New Zealand, Canada, Newfoundland and South Africa. Black Africans took part in the earliest military actions by British land forces of the First World War. Empire forces went on to make significant contributions to British efforts on the widespread fighting fronts, including France, Belgium, Egypt, Palestine, Salonika, Macedonia and Mesopotamia. By 1918 the Indian Army had grown from 150,000 in 1914 to 1.4 million men in total who served during the war. It was a racially and religiously diverse force, and also included 100,000 Gurkhas joining its ranks from Nepal. Thousands of men travelled from Jamaica, Trinidad and Tobago, Barbados, the Bahamas, Grenada and the many other Caribbean islands that formed the British West Indies at that time.

Hundreds of thousands of non-white men joined imperial labour units to undertake strenuous repair and maintenance work in support of the British war effort. Labourers were often treated with contempt. A sense of racial hierarchy was deeply entrenched at this time. The South African government recruited 20,000 volunteers into the South African Native Labour Corps on the understanding that they would not mix with white soldiers. They spent most of their service unable to leave specially designated camps unless they were working. Over half a million men served with the Indian Labour Corps on the various fighting fronts. Around 100,000 men were recruited from China (neutral until the country joined the war in 1917) into the Chinese Labour Corps.

Wherever they were from, labour units undertook vital duties to grease the wheels of the war machine. They carried munitions, mended trenches, cooked meals for the troops, repaired mechanical vehicles and carried the wounded to medical help, among other tasks. Although most labourers worked behind the front line, they suffered major losses. Many

died on arduous journeys over the sea before even reaching war zones; others died from illness after they arrived or were killed by long-range shellfire or by German air raids, or in accidents attributable to faulty shells. In all, around one-quarter of the million men who died defending the British Empire during the conflict came from countries other than Britain and Ireland.

An Indian Lewis gun team fires at an enemy aircraft on the Mesopotamian Front in 1918; other soldiers run for cover into slit trenches. Over 29,000 Indian soldiers perished during this long campaign.

THEATRES OF WAR

On the Western Front effective ways of killing were constantly sought in the hope of achieving a breakthrough. The fighting was both technically pioneering and yet at times oddly medieval in its methods. Driving men

Right: Men from the British West Indies stack shells at a dump at Ypres, October 1917. 'Native' troops, as they were then called, were used primarily for labouring tasks, from moving shells to repairing trenches.

Below right: George V inspecting men from the South African Native Labour Corps at Abbeville, France in 1917. Labourers from the British Empire provided essential manpower to the British forces, but many experienced systematic racial discrimination during their service.

from their positions demanded an arsenal of weapons, ranging from the modern to the antediluvian –poison gas, sniper rifles, grenades and trench mortars combined with knives, clubs, bayonets and revolvers for close combat. Tunnellers worked deep under the earth to lay mines, capable of wiping out hundreds of men in a moment.

Certain battles exemplified the war's devastating loss of life. For Britain, this was epitomised by the Battle of the Somme, most especially its deadly first day on 1 July 1916. At 7.30am on that sunny Saturday British troops emerged from their trenches and advanced across no man's land towards the German lines. The 19,240 fatalities remain the worst ever suffered by the British Army in a single day – one in five of those then in action. The battle lasted for five gruelling months.

The war at sea was no less brutal. British naval power had been the supreme symbol of national might in the Edwardian age, its imposing Dreadnought battleships rendering all other vessels obsolete. These revolutionary vessels were the result of a naval arms race in the years leading up to the First World War between Britain and Germany. Despite this feverish shipbuilding, the war at sea never delivered the decisive encounter that each side desired. Instead ships and submarines waged a merciless war of blockade to try and starve the other side into surrender. Thousands of men died in submarines, ripped open by depth charges or mines deep under the waves. Torpedoed naval and merchant ships sank swiftly, bringing many others to a cold, watery grave. Only once did British and German battleships clash in a significant sea battle, off Jutland in 1916. Within hours some 6,000 British and nearly 3,000 German sailors were dead; most had drowned in the North Sea.

The air war provided a deadly new dimension of conflict. The first heavier-than-air flight had taken place barely over a decade before the war began. Increasingly sophisticated aeroplanes were deployed in combat, flying over the trenches to direct artillery fire and take reconnaissance photographs. As the aircraft improved, the air war grew in scope and intensity. Airmen bombed and shot at soldiers and sites beneath them. Fighter pilots duelled in the air, with those who racked up multiple kills – the 'air aces' – becoming feted as celebrities.

Despite the perceived glamour of aerial warfare, it posed a lethal threat to pilots. Fragile aircraft were prone to mechanical failure, and fear of dying in a fiery inferno troubled even the most experienced airmen. Some carried pistols with which to take their own lives if the worst happened. As on land, the air war soon degenerated into an attritional struggle, killing men at a prodigious rate. British pilots lasted an average of ten weeks before being shot down. Flying provoked a particularly intense fear, with many men referring to the onset of this anxiety as getting 'the wind up'. An anonymous pilot's diary, written during his training in 1918, gave an insight into this, observing:

Previous page: Italian troops armed with skis move up through a snow-clad pass in blizzard conditions. The war's diverse theatres spanned mountains, deserts, flat countryside, the sea and the air.

The sinking of the British troopship SS *Arcadian* cost nearly 300 lives after the vessel was torpedoed by a German submarine following its departure from the Salonika Front. This dramatic photograph shows men sliding down ropes to escape.

I am on tenter-hooks all the time I am up, and dare not for the life of me climb to 3,000 feet, getting most terrible wind up as soon as I reach 1200 and I shall be in France next month, so God help me.

A few weeks later, the same pilot noted his concerns about his aircraft:

Only I shall probably kill myself on these RE8s. However, I had far better kill myself than resign my commission and become a ranker.

While it is impossible to know the extent to which soldiers, sailors and airmen worried about the fate of their flesh, the vast majority marshalled the mental stamina to carry out their orders despite the very real threat of death. The ability to function came from a desire to not 'let the side down'. Men looked to one another for emotional support, often through gallows humour. Others had to force down their own fear, as recalled in later years by Signaller Arthur Winstanley, who

Left: The body of Lieutenant Paul Denys Montague in front of his aircraft after he was shot down on the Salonika Front in October 1917. Lieutenant Montague was subsequently buried at the crash site. Pilots and airmen faced extreme danger from both enemy fire and mechanical failure.

Below left: A rare 'air to air' photograph of a Royal Flying Corps BE2c aircraft in flight over trench lines in 1916. Such were the dangers from guns on the ground, the planes were also forced to carry out their missions at higher altitude to avoid being struck.

described German shelling by 'Jerry', the term used by many British soldiers for the Germans:

> Gerry [*sic*] by now was thoroughly awake, he started shelling our front line, it was awful. The chap who was to partner me was crying like a frightened baby, on the firestep. He had lost his nerve completely. I didn't treat him gently, I cursed him madly, and pointed out that the lads had gone over, so we would have to stand to <u>our</u> duty. If I had talked gently to him, in those conditions I would have lost my own nerve.

While the possibility of violent death was ever-present, the conditions in which servicemen and women lived also rendered everyone susceptible to disease and fatal accidents. The war's final death tolls were grossly inflated by terminal damage caused by faulty shells, the spread of diseases such as malaria or succumbing to pneumonia and similar conditions. The trying conditions in which ailments were suffered often rendered recovery impossible.

With so many dead, British rituals of remembrance came to reflect the sheer enormity of this 'total war'. The conflict's scale had been shown in its tremendous demand for men, munitions and money, its political upheavals, the interdependence of the home and fighting fronts, the threat to national survival and the escalating human cost. From mantelpiece memorials to state-sponsored monuments, an industry of remembrance iconography revealed itself in hundreds of thousands of homes and within the civic fabric of Britain itself. Remembrance of the British war dead was to be crucially influenced by decisions made about the logistical challenges posed by the dead and the missing. But first the news of death had to be communicated – and endured.

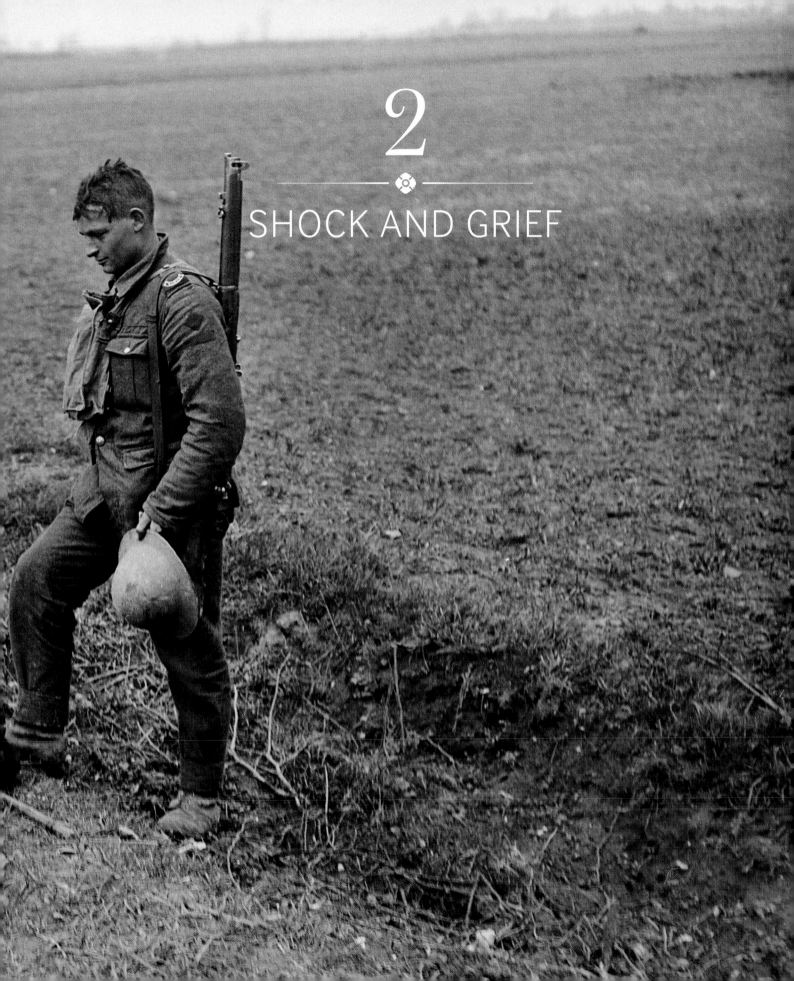

2

❋

SHOCK AND GRIEF

Fears about the safe return of loved ones from the fighting fronts were not misplaced. Deaths in action or through tragic accidents, fatalities from grievous wounds or the onset of disease claimed nearly one million British and Empire lives. Some three-quarters of a million men from Britain and Ireland died. Yet it is true that nearly nine out of ten servicemen survived the war and returned back to Britain, rendering allusions to a 'lost generation' of British men statistically untrue at the broadest level. The permutations of loss between social classes gave a genuine basis to a notion that the upper classes had been disproportionately affected. Certainly the casualties among officers, trained as they were to lead from the front, were very high. Although working class rank and file soldiers were more numerous, the need to retain labour in industry also kept many at home. The idea that an 'elite' of men in their prime had been wiped out gathered traction after the war, with many acts of remembrance paying tribute to this so-called 'lost generation'.

However the complex demographic patterns of death played out, nothing tempered the individual experience of a direct bereavement. Every death extinguished a unique personality, severing a source of practical support as well as emotional sustenance. In becoming a soldier, sailor, airman, nurse or any role that drew one near to enemy weapons, the potential for death had to be faced. It is impossible to quantify the extent to which servicemen and women accepted the risk to their own lives, nor how intense fears were in households across Britain that their loved ones would not return. The fact that many citizen soldiers had actively chosen to face danger by 'joining up' voluntarily added deeper resonance to the nation's burgeoning grief.

Britain was unique among all the combatant nations in having a voluntary system of army recruitment upon the outbreak of the First World War. In 1914 men were invited, persuaded and later pressured to 'join up' for the duration of the 'emergency' – and the associated threat to life that this entailed. In the early weeks of the conflict, hundreds of thousands of civilians committed themselves on oath to serve 'King and Country'. They become soldiers amidst an exuberant atmosphere of 'war fever'. Yet these decisions, often made on the spur of the moment, had dramatic ramifications for families. While some were desperately proud of their relative's decision to serve, others immediately began to worry. Mill worker Kitty Morter was aghast when her husband Percy was recruited during a night out at the Palace Theatre in Manchester in 1914 to see the renowned entertainer Vesta Tilley:

> But what we didn't know until we got there was that also on stage were Army officers with tables all set out for recruiting...Then she [Tilley] came off the stage and walked all round the audience – up and down, either sides, down the middle – and the young men were getting up and following her. When she got to our row she hesitated a bit. I don't quite

know what happened but she put her hand on my husband's shoulder – he was on the end seat – and as the men were all following her, he got up and followed her too.

When we got home that night I was terribly upset. I told him I didn't want him to go and be a soldier – I didn't want to lose him. I didn't want him to go at all. But he said, 'We have to go. There has to be men to go'.

Whatever their role, whether chosen freely or imposed by compulsory conscription from 1916, millions of British people were drawn into military service. The majority of fatalities were soldiers on the Western Front. Here relentless bloody actions took place, from the earliest days of the war in August 1914 until the declaration of a ceasefire in November 1918. Deaths that came in the war's dying days were an especially cruel blow for the families of long-serving soldiers who had endured so many twists and turns during the war.

BREAKING THE NEWS

Whenever a death occurred, it was confirmed in a relatively formulaic manner. Commanding officers led roll calls after each action, although these proved inexact in accounting for human resources. Eyewitness accounts from survivors captured details about the last known movements of the 'missing'. Caught up in battlefield chaos, some men were prematurely presumed dead. This was the case for Lieutenant Hugh Bird, who served on the Western Front from June 1917 until March 1918. A War Office telegram incorrectly notified his family of his death in action in March 1918. A letter from Bird's Commanding Officer to his brother laid plain the chaos of the action in which he was presumed to have died:

I wrote about a month ago to your brother's wife telling her all I could – which, I am so sorry to say, was very little. We were fighting a very hard rear-guard action when your brother was killed by a shell. That is practically all I can tell you. In fighting a rear-guard action it is very, very difficult to get even one's wounded back – the gallant boys who are killed cannot possibly be looked after and buried; they simply have to be left where they fall. This was your brother's fate, and I can only hope that the clearing parties of the enemy buried him and have marked his grave. He did the same for the enemy when <u>they</u> were retiring and I think we can take it for granted they are doing the same for us. If this is so, information will come through one day as to where he is buried.

Lieutenant Bird's obituary was published in May in the *L and N W Gazette*. However, it later transpired that he was not dead at all – he had been captured and held as a prisoner at Ohrdruf in Germany.

The opposite scenario, in which dead men were initially described as 'missing', was painfully common. Sometimes it took months to confirm that the worst had actually happened. Families were left in suspense, often exerting considerable energy in their dealings with officialdom to try and confirm the fate of a loved one. This process continued beyond the war's end, but it was sometimes only possible to presume, rather than corroborate, a death. The family of Lance Corporal Nelson Newman, for example, were left in turmoil for a year and a half before receiving the formal decree:

> It is my painful duty to inform you that no further news having been received relative to (No.) 9289 (Rank) Lance Corporal (Name) Nelson Newman (Regiment) 4th R. Fus. who has been missing since 26th Oct. 1914, the Army Council have been regretfully constrained to conclude that he is dead, and that his death took place on the 26th Oct. 1914 (or since).

Whether met with stoical acceptance or shocked despair, reactions to news of a death back home were as individual as the life lost. The news was reported home by way of formal telegram to the next of kin, and these rudimentary notes set in motion a family's grief. The telegrams contained the most perfunctory information about the date, place and nature of the death, and whether a man had been killed in action, died later from wounds or from illness.

Every death splintered a family, whether relationships were close or distant. The ripples of each loss spread far – many were boyfriends, brothers, husbands; some were fathers. Some were teenagers who had slipped through the military recruitment system as underage volunteers. Extended families were also battered by bereavement, as interactions between aunts, uncles, nieces and nephews could be as dependent as any parent or sibling tie. Friendship was a less formal orbit than family, but losses were no less significant for that; grieving mates were also affected by the death of their old friends. Given that childhood pals were often scattered across disparate fighting fronts on active services, all at risk of meeting the same fate, many remained unaware for some time that their friends had been killed.

Surviving letters and diaries, and retrospective interview recollections by those who received news of a wartime death, provide glimpses into profoundly varied reactions. Whether those affected were sanguine and fully accepting of the consequences of active service, or knocked sideways in shock and despair, each death opened up the same question – was the war worth the loss?

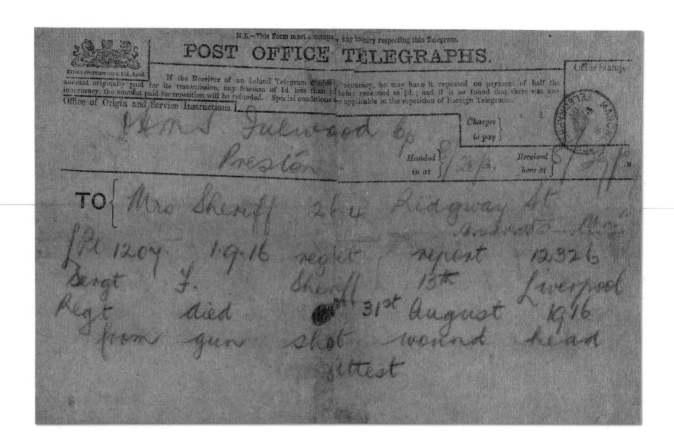

Kitty Morter was six months pregnant when her husband Percy was killed on the Somme in July 1916. Her grief produced a suicidal despair three months later upon the birth of her son, whom she named Percy after his father:

During the time that he was away I was very, very lonely as I didn't make friends very easily. And all the thoughts I had was for my husband. Times was very, very hard and I only had 12s and 6d a week and therefore I couldn't go out and spend like anyone else. And I used to sit at night and try to do a bit of reading to pass the time away like that. But it was very, very hard and I would wonder what he was doing and if he was thinking about me. And wondering how he was going on and when I would see him again. And all things like that. So, after I found that it was officially known that he had been killed I used to pass my time away trying to make little baby clothes for my baby and eventually the baby came to be born. It was born at home, but I don't remember it being born at all. I had a very bad time. I had two doctors and I don't remember the baby being born. And I felt I didn't want to live. I'd no wish to live at all because the world had come to an end then, for me, because I'd lost all that I'd loved.

Telegrams conveyed the news of a death back to the home front. This example from August 1916 advised Sergeant Frederick Sheriff's next of kin in the starkest terms that he had died from a gunshot wound to the head the day before on the Western Front.

Following the death of Lance Corporal Ammon Whitehead on the Gallipoli Front, his wife Winnie was incapacitated with grief. In a letter she described the return of his possessions:

> His diary was in the package – carefully filled in to Aug 30th. The last words were shall see docks to-morrow – all night 7 p.m. I had the parcel a day before I dare open it – and when I found the diary, with the record of all the voyage, and what he had been through till the 30th I read – with a sick heart till midnight, & then went to bed – thinking – this is the limit – I can endure no more.

Later, with the help of a doctor, she made a recovery:

> I am feeling very much stronger & recognise the wisdom of the dr's orders to stay in bed & see people there quietly. I seem to wake & doze all the nights through, having the happiest times with Ammon. The dear boy fell a long way off in Gallipoli, but now he's so close. I am able to look after mother as usual now – she was getting very fagged.

In the midst of grief and loss over a man's death, domestic responsibilities for family members fell more heavily than ever on women. This was particularly the case for widows left to raise children.

LAYING THE DEAD TO REST

After sustaining a fatal wound, life could end in an instant, after hours writhing in agony or as a release after months of steady decline. Men died raiding enemy trenches; storming across no man's land; curled up in their dug outs; while devouring their rations; pacing along duckboards; unconscious in sleep. The end might come through devastating wounds that proved deadly far from the battlefield itself, in hospital beds miles from the front line or after a man had been brought back to Britain for treatment. Later in the war pits were dug before major actions in anticipation of the bodies with which they would soon be filled.

Over these rugged resting places, army padres conducted short services wherever possible to mark committal to the earth. In an interview many years later Private Reginald Glenn described a rudimentary service that took place in the winter of 1916 in the Somme area:

Our chaplain, I used to go about with him with a little organ and I used to play the organ for little services, and one day the chaplain and another officer took me out into no man's land, where our troops had all gone forward then and taken Serre village, and what we'd tried to do before, and we stood there with all these skeletons lying around and this officer said to the chaplain, 'Can we sing a little hymn over these bodies?' and so the three of us stood there and we sang the hymn 'On the Resurrection Morning'. And then the next morning I know it snowed heavily and it covered all the bodies over.

Army chaplains from the Church of England, Roman Catholic Church and the Presbyterian Church attend the burial of four British soldiers at Gallipoli in 1915. The army tried to provide a chaplain from the relevant faith to preside over burials, but this was far from always possible.

Army chaplain Reverend Ernest Crosse presided over many makeshift funerals as well as more formal services:

When battalions returned to rest after battle it was usual to hold a service of Thanksgiving if a victory had been won, and in any case a Memorial Service for those who had been killed. Both services were often most impressive and the great sense of reverence, of which one could be certain, quite justified the

A plaque commemorating Sergeant Raymond Simpkin, who died of his wounds on 5 May 1916. His brother (also a serving soldier) erected an elaborately decorated wooden grave marker in the Somme area, made from intricately woven rope and metal leaves and flowers. The plaque read simply: 'From Sgt A. Simpkin in loving memory of my dear brother, Sgt R. Simpkin.'

experiment sometimes made of making the Memorial Service a Requiem. 'We also bless Thy holy name for all thy servants departed this life in thy faith and fear.' It seemed so perfectly appropriate. We have no desire to enter into religious controversy, but it was one of the few assets of the war that it revived the pious practice of praying for the dead...

Helmets were sometimes placed tenderly upon freshly dug graves, or rifles speared into the ground to act as informal markers and tributes. Second Lieutenant Roland Ingle described a lovingly tended burial site on the Somme, in which he was later laid to rest himself, a few days after writing:

The graves are beautifully kept, and the crosses made in various patterns, all carefully done by the pioneer battalion who are responsible for these things. Often you see figures or inscriptions carved in chalk placed on the graves, or, on the cross itself, the dead man's cap. Often there are flowers, and men – pals from the dead man's company – tending the graves.

When possible, grieving soldiers left tributes to dead comrades. This personalised temporary grave marker for Lieutenant Alan Lloyd provides an emphatic tribute to his character: HE DIED AS HE LIVED. BRAVE AND FEARLESS. A TRUE BRITISH HERO.

Amateur horticultural tributes were also attempted, as recounted by Lance Corporal Noel Galt. He wrote a letter to the father of Private Warwick Squire:

> He is buried in the field behind the trenches amongst the others, and his grave is planted with Lilies of the Valley and Daffodils which we got from a deserted garden and has a little shrub at each corner. We made it as nice as we could, but I'm afraid it isn't very grand.

Temporary wooden grave markers were part of official attempts to keep order to the business of mass burial. But they were also a common means of expressing individual tributes to fellow soldiers. Simple crosses were scrawled with compassionate words. On 4 August 1916 Lieutenant Alan Lloyd was hit by a shell while serving on the Somme. He was buried nearby the next day. Gunner John Manning was with Lloyd when he was killed. Several weeks later he placed a simple sign on Lloyd's grave (see opposite).

It was very occasionally possible for family members to visit graves if they were also in the forces. Signaller Stapleton Eachus recorded consecutive attempts in his diary (on 1 and 3 April 1917) to pay tribute to his cousin's husband during a break from normal duties:

> Rose shortly after 7am and after breakfast I proceeded on foot to Corbie for the purpose of buying a wreath to place on the grave of 2nd Lt. Santler, the late husband of my cousin Isabel Brown. I reached the shop at about 9.45am and after inspecting the number of wreaths I chose one composed of roses of a celluloid composition. The colours include cream, white, pink (light and darker) shades, red and deep red. These are the best descriptions I can give of the colours. A rosette of red, white and blue ribbon about 4 inches in width is attached. The inscription which I request be affixed to the wreath is composed of aluminium characters of between 1½ and 2 inches in height arranged in four rows across the wreath in the following manner '2nd Lt. SANTLER FROM HIS LOVING WIFE ISABEL AND ALL WHO LOVED HIM'.

Two days later, he noted:

> I arrived at the graveside about midday. Snow still partly covered the earth. The soil upon the grave was somewhat disarranged, which looked as though small heaps of earth had been tumbled upon the whole plot. I did my best to rearrange the surface with my hands, which was however not an easy matter, owing to the clayey nature of the soil, which was at the time quite waterlogged in consequence of the thaw, which had set in during the morning. I hung Isabel's wreath upon the cross by means of a hook, but finding that the wind

would probably ruin it entirely in a short space of time, by blowing it about,
I bound the wreath to the cross by means of some thin cable wire, which I
fortunately found close at hand.

A BAND OF BROTHERS

Sparring wit, songs and shared slang forged a true sense of ragged
togetherness between servicemen. Even the dependable irritations of
each other's habits in claustrophobic circumstances, from snoring to
snapping at one another, contributed to this bond. There was often an
intensity to these connections created by the fragility of life under fire.
This also included relationships between British soldiers and French
civilians who lived in war zones, according to Signaller Stapleton Eachus
in a diary entry for 1916: 'It is perfectly true that there have been quite a
large number of marriages contracted between the "lily" and the "rose",
and in addition a vast number of unsolomnised unions also.'

Emotional responses to a loss were not just reserved for men of similar
rank. The disciplinary and class divide between officers and the men they
commanded, especially in the war's early years, was often bridged by the
war's extreme demands. Lieutenant E W Stoneham recalled:

> The comradeship amongst men was really most extraordinary and very
> difficult to describe. On one occasion I was offered a safe job behind the
> lines if I would care to join Brigade Headquarters. It was very tempting,
> but I didn't want to go. There was something about the relationship with
> the men that one didn't want to break. One would somehow have felt
> rather a traitor to them, so I refused it and stayed with them. Somehow
> one had a very strong sense of belonging – to the men and to the job.

Burying their comrades was an understandable strain upon
soldiers. But Ernest Crosse recalled another tension evident at burials
on the Western Front:

> As one looked on the weary band of tired and muddy comrades who had
> come to fulfil this last duty to their friend, one felt, in a way one seldom does
> at an ordinary funeral, that there was a sense in which they really were to be
> envied, since for them the long-drawn out agony of war was at an end.

While many attempts were made to mark and mourn lost friends and
comrades, grief was more often than not smothered by an avalanche of

A British soldier wearing a sheepskin coat embraces a French farm girl under a sprig of mistletoe shortly before Christmas in 1917. Relationships often flourished between soldiers and local civilians on the Western Front during breaks from fighting behind the lines.

daily drudgery. Going into action was a far more exceptional event than the constant toil of repairing trenches, carrying food supplies up the line, attempting to keep clean in squalid conditions, snatching hours of sleep and spending exhausting hours on the march. Anguish, loss and the fear of sudden death found more toxic ways of revealing themselves. The sense of cohesion in a unit might start to disintegrate as new troops stepped into the place of the dead, leading to brittle tempers and strained nerves. Yet there was, for many, little time during the war to dwell on the lives lost. Lieutenant Stewart Montagu Cleeve recalled:

> We found we literally couldn't walk along the trenches without treading on dead bodies, German and British. The stench and the flies were simply appalling. That was one of the most miserable memories I have of the Somme. It was pathetic really. Eventually one just got over it and thought nothing of it. We couldn't help it, we were alive and that's what mattered. And being alive, we jolly well had to get on with it.

Shared bonds within units formed early in the war eroded with every fatality and unit reshuffling, although the entire military system was designed to foster a spirit capable of retaining its fighting fitness throughout the conflict, as Lieutenant-Colonel Alfred Irwin remembered:

There was a very strong battalion feeling. The chaps we got were gradually getting nearer and nearer to the dregs of the nation, of course, but they all seemed to become 8th East Surreys in an extraordinary short length of time.

A smiling group of Gordon Highlanders in a reserve trench in France in November 1916. Bonds of comradeship were often strong and, despite the prevalence of death, the loss of an individual soldier could deeply distress those who had lived and fought alongside him.

LETTERS OF CONDOLENCE

After a death, it was usual practice for a commanding officer to write a letter of condolence to the next of kin as soon as a moment presented itself to do so. After a particularly bloody action this could prove a sizeable task, exerting a heavy toll on the officer responsible. Letters were also written by military chaplains, who increasingly spent a great deal of their time with men at the front line. Reverend Ernest Crosse reflected at length about the contribution made by padres in writing these difficult letters:

28 Nov 1917

Dear Mr Campion,

I expect that before this letter reaches you the sad news will have been conveyed to you about your son Pte A Campion (37780) who was killed in action on 16th of this month, but I must write to you and express my deep sympathy with you and your family in your great loss.

We are faced with so much sorrow in these days but still each fresh casualty brings its special grief to some household and I know how little one can do to comfort those who mourn the loss of their dear ones. At the same time I believe it is the case that a letter from one who has been with the Battalion so long as I have and who can speak of the excellent tone of the men and their fine record all through does bring with it some little comfort.

Your son together with three of his companions was waiting to make an attack that evening (16th) when a shell fell right on the top of them and killed them all instantaneously. They would not have known anything about it. They were buried as true soldiers - on the battlefield - the only thing that was possible their souls we commit

Left and opposite: Army chaplain Reverend Arthur Longden wrote this condolence letter to the parents of Private Arthur Campion, who was killed in action, aged 20, on 16 November 1917. Longden hoped that his words would bring 'some little comfort' to Campion's parents in England.

If an officer was killed the C.O. and usually one or more of his company officers were pretty sure to write to his home and give details. But in the case of other ranks this was by no means always the case. Thousands and thousands must have been killed on active service under circumstances which were perfectly well-known to their comrades, while next-of-kin received nothing more than the cold official fact notified to them by the War Office. This scanty information a padre could often forestall, and usually supplement by the addition of a few details, which made just all the difference to the man's home. After a big action, when possibly two or three hundred in the padre's two battalions were killed, it

> into the hands of our Heavenly Father. may
> He comfort you & all who mourn the loss
> of this faithful son of the Empire
>
> I am
> yours sincerely
> Arthur Longsden
> Chaplain
> 8th Ry Berks Regt

was impossible to give very many details, but on these occasions I always used to print off a circular letter, giving such general details of the action as were permissible, and adding in some cases such details as I had time for. How much these letters were appreciated only the mourners can fully realise.

Be they from a commanding officer, chaplain or comrade, condolence letters varied in tone: they might be perfunctory, polite or overtly patriotic. Many exuded a compelling, almost paternal affection for the deceased if a commanding officer had taken a keen interest in the morale and welfare of his men. These communications were retained by families as a form of memorial, a testament to their loved one's significance in the national emergency and a source of bittersweet pride. But Reverend Crosse explained some of the pitfalls of the exercise:

> Experience showed that one had to be very careful in writing these letters, and it was well to keep a duplicate of them. Accuracy was essential, and it was quite rightly forbidden in any way to go beyond the official announcement as to the man's fate. For instance, if a man were reported officially merely as 'missing', it was absolutely forbidden to say 'that he might be presumed to have been killed', or, in the case of the dead, that, if he had lived, 'he would probably have been awarded a decoration'. The reasons for these restrictions, hard as they may seem, were obvious when one came to think over the matter. In very few cases had the writer any personal knowledge of those to whom he was writing, and though nearly all took the letter simply for what it was, a mark of sympathy, some few did not scruple to use such letters as a ground for making claims on The War Office.

> It is not without interest to note the type of reply which these letters produced and after a time I came to classify them under four heads: -

> A.   Those which were merely letters of thanks.

> B.   Those which in addition to the thanks asked for further particulars of a kind, which, if time permitted, one might be able to add.

> C.   Replies which asked for impossible details, usually concerned with the dead man's estate or effects.

> D.   A very small minority which showed no gratitude. Some of these suggested that I was personally responsible for every article which it was assumed the man was carrying at the time of his death. One even threatened me with legal proceedings because I had been unable to bury the man's body.

The wife of Lance Corporal Ernest Nicholson from Stockport received one such consoling missive. Aged 32 and the father of a one-year-old son, he was killed in action during the Third Battle of Ypres in 1917. Three days later Nicholson's widow Jessie received these words:

> The death has taken from my squadron one of the most hardworking and conscientious of the Military Mounted Police in my squadron. He was liked and

respected by both officer and men of the squadron. Your husband suffered no pain, as he was killed instantaneously by a fragment of a shell which exploded near him. He is buried in a military cemetery near here. An army chaplain read the burial service, and his troop officer was also present. All ranks join with me in tendering to you our deepest sympathy with you in your sad loss.

This letter to Mrs Nicholson mirrored so many thousands written by commanding officers in its expressions of sympathy, the respect felt by his unit, the loss his death had inflicted upon it and notification of a burial when a body had been recovered to make this possible. Its stark but reassuring details about the pain-free, instantaneous manner of his death was one of the most well-worn consolation lines written in the hundreds of thousands of letters sent back to grieving families in Britain. Some correspondents made great efforts to reassure families that the war's purpose was succour in itself. Private John Douglas Tomlinson's mother received a letter from Captain Houghton following his death in October 1917:

He was always cheerful, even under most trying circumstances, and in this way did much to keep up the spirits of the men in No. 7 Platoon.

But take comfort in this, that he died a brave soldier's death in a magnificent cause.

Consolation was also channelled through a bitter hatred of the enemy, again giving some sense that the loss was worthwhile. The brother of Lieutenant Gerald Renny received a letter from a man in the same battery after Renny was killed, aged 21, on 15 April 1917:

He was such a cheerful lad & quite irresistible as a pal. It is hard that he had to go when so many rotters still live. I have always hated the Boche but now I shall have a very deep personal score to pay back, and by God he shall get it every time I sit down to measure an angle!

All of these letters were written while the war carried on. At such a time personal grief – while consuming – always played second fiddle to the requirements of the war at the front. However, the logistics of dealing with death and burial on such a vast and relentless scale became an unprecedented practical challenge for the authorities. This would lead to profound, sometimes inflammatory decisions that went on to shape how Britain's war dead were commemorated when the fighting finally stopped.

3

DEALING WITH THE DEAD

B efore the First World War, only the military dead with the clout of Horatio Nelson could expect to be returned to Britain for burial. Following the Admiral's death in 1805 at the Battle of Trafalgar his remains – pickled in brandy for preservation during the voyage – were returned on board HMS *Victory* for a grand state funeral in London. The contrast with the army rank and file during wars of the nineteenth century could not be greater. They could expect to be interred abroad in unmarked mass graves.

Bodies, body parts and the unaccounted for 'missing' posed tremendous logistical, moral and psychological challenges for every combatant nation during the First World War. The brutal effectiveness of powerful weaponry resulted in many men being dismembered, obliterated, buried under tonnes of violently disturbed earth or drowned. But very quickly a wholesale change in previously dismissive attitudes towards the death of the lower ranks set in. It rapidly became unacceptable to gloss over the death of an army private, especially as most British soldiers had been coaxed, or in later years forced, into taking temporary leave from their normal lives for the 'national emergency'. Popular support for the war effort was dependent on the recognition of 'citizen soldiers'.

RETRIEVAL AND BURIAL

Identifying the whereabouts and names of the dead in the aftermath of a battle allowed commanders to assess and reorganise their fighting strength accordingly. But a more nebulous issue was at stake too: the maintenance of good morale and military effectiveness. Heavy casualties might be accepted if they were incurred during a successful action that saw real territorial gains. A limited number of deaths could have a corrosive effect if survivors believed that lives of their comrades had been thrown away uselessly. Servicemen also needed to know that the wounded would be cared for and the dead properly treated. The authorities feared that the sight of decomposing comrades had the potential to incite despair, anguish and fear. The Reverend Ernest Crosse, an army chaplain who conducted hundreds of burials on the Western Front, described their significance:

> In the first place if one had buried a man's body one knew for certain that he was dead. The compiling of really accurate casualty lists was from every point of view a most important matter, and after an action a padre could do a work of immense importance in identifying and burying the dead, and reporting what he had done to his battalion H.Q. Secondly nothing is more depressing to the living than to see unburied

Right: British dead being prepared for a mass burial, April 1918.

Below right: Stretcher bearers carry a wounded soldier past recently killed British soldiers during the Battle of Amiens on 9 August 1918.

Gathering the Dead for Burial by Harry Bateman, Thiepval Wood, 1916. This pencil drawing portrays a burial party collecting another body behind a pile of human remains in the foreground

dead around them. In some areas, e.g. at Beaumont Hamel in the winter of 1916, the ground was covered with unburied dead, and it became a matter of real military importance that the work of burial should be conducted. But it was no easy matter ... to do so without getting fresh casualties among the burial party...

The dangers encountered by such parties were very real, but those involved were compelled – and determined – to undertake their duties thoroughly upon the discovery of fallen comrades, as Reverend Crosse explained:

The discovery and identification of the body settled a man's fate beyond all question, and the sooner this was done after the action took place the more accurate and complete the casualty list would be. It was worth almost any amount of labour to avoid reporting a man as 'missing' unnecessarily.

It was also considered essential to bury human remains promptly where possible to maintain vital public support back in Britain. If news spread that scores of dead bodies had been left strewn across and abandoned on battlefields, this could imperil the productivity of the home front and its commitment to winning the war.

Where human remains were recovered in the war's early stages, graves were usually dug close to where men had died. These burials were often conducted in haste, in ground that was to be fought over repeatedly throughout the war in a pendulum of destruction. Shalllow graves might prove temporary resting places, as trench digging and artillery barrages frequently unearthed corpses.

As the war's bloodiness amplified, the practical challenges grew exponentially. Every theatre of war was affected, but problems became most pressing on the Western Front. Here the greatest number of casualties were sustained in trench warfare, in which hundreds of front line infantry soldiers were often required to face enemy fire to make diminutive territorial gains at great human cost. Efforts were made to retrieve bodies, but this often proved impossible, as Reverend Crosse discovered during his work on the front line:

> Difficulties of various kinds sometimes arose about burials. I remember one distinguished general who, on seeing a large number of unburied dead in front of our line, roundly abused me for not having done my job. I answered him in the only possible way by telling him that, though I should much like to bury the dead, I reckoned it was impossible to do so without adding to their number, whereupon he quite changed his tone and added 'well, padre, I expect you know your job better than I do'. Sometimes of course it was quite impossible to collect a burial party. Usually however this was only a question of a padre being on the spot and choosing the right time, and 'the right time' was very much a matter of experience. In a big battle the task might be very difficult. If it was successful and our line advanced there was certain to be a short period when the enemy artillery were moving back to new positions and this interlude provided an excellent chance if one took it at once. If the battle was a failure the task was far harder as enemy artillery were in the same position and were sure to be strafing heavily to prevent reinforcements coming up.

There had been no official preparations for dealing with bodies on the scale that came to pass. While commanding a unit of British Red Cross support drivers in 1914, 45-year-old Fabian Ware became concerned by the magnitude of fatalities and the lack of coordinated information about their resting places. His unit began to record details about the jumble of unsystematic grave locations. Ware's unit's pioneering work, in the difficult and chaotic circumstances of an ongoing war, was recognised and his unit was officially subsumed into the army in 1915. The new

Graves Registration Commission now became responsible for finding, marking and registering graves, and the identities of their occupants if possible. Where feasible, its units rationalised the scattered human remains of British and Empire soldiers into larger cemeteries. Their duties were described in detail in the recollections of Reginald Bryan, who worked for Ware's Red Cross Unit and subsequently with the Graves Registration Commission:

> In a nutshell our chief work is to identify and register the graves of British soldiers who have fallen. This may seem an apparently easy task, but on investigation it is not so easy as it looks. In the base cemeteries and those behind the lines, it is comparatively easy to mark the graves with crosses bearing the name, regiment, etc., of those who have died. The difficulty is when the soldiers are buried in fields, or orchards, sometimes singly and sometimes several graves together. The graves are generally marked by a rough wooden cross, probably erected by a sorrowing comrade with the name and other particulars on the cross. The French people are very good in a lot of districts, attending to the graves and taking flowers to lay on them. I have no doubt it arouses their sympathy to think that these brave fellows

Left: A dedication ceremony for Bailleul Military Cemetery, December 1915. The event was attended by members of a Graves Registration Unit including Reginald Bryan, who wrote an account of his burial work during the war and whose presence in the photograph is indicated by his inititials 'R.H.B.'.

Below left: British soldiers search the body of a soldier for official identification discs or personal items – from pocket-sized photographs to shaving mirrors – that might be inscribed with his name in France, 10 August 1918.

have laid down their lives and are buried under a foreign sky, and their bereaved relatives, it may be, will never be able to visit the last resting-place of their loved ones. All these temporary crosses are replaced by our crosses: that is, plain wooden crosses with metal inscriptions on them. Of course many of our soldiers are buried close to the lines, and it is often impossible to get to them for some little time, but this is obviously quite unavoidable.

In the first few months of the war, during the famous retreat from Mons and the more famous victories on the Aisne and Marne, it was inevitable that many were buried in fields or on farms and in other such places; but since the trench warfare commenced an endeavour has been made to bury all soldiers in cemeteries, either civil or military, which of course makes the work of identification much simpler.

Although naturally we can do very little indeed to relieve the distress and sorrow caused by the death of husbands, brothers and friends in this war, it may be, and indeed is, a solace to the relatives to know that the graves are marked and, as far as possible, are being cared for. Our efforts will undoubtedly come into more prominence after the war, when large numbers of relatives will certainly come over here to see the graves and have them cared for. You would be surprised if you saw how nice some of the military cemeteries are being kept.

Coping strategies for those retrieving the bodies were also noted by Bryan:

It was really melancholy work and a rather sad task, but it was a necessary one, as apart from its sentimental value, it was necessary from a sanitary point of view. However, we didn't go about with long faces but tried to keep as cheerful and jolly as we could.

Frozen ground during severe winters made it difficult to inter bodies properly, as did the dangers of setting foot into no man's land to retrieve the dead. Hindrances and hazards resulted in the most superficial of burials, as Lieutenant George Craike recalled:

We crawled out of the trenches with caution in small parties, and dealt with the dead by simply pulling them into depressions in the earth, or into shell holes. This was not a pleasant task and occasionally the arms disengaged from the bodies. However, the bodies were placed as far as possible in these holes and covered over with a light layer of earth, this earth being brushed or dug in by the entrenching tools. All the work had to be done on all fours, for to stand erect was courting disaster. In addition the very frequent lights of the Germans necessitated instant stillness while these lights illuminated in the sky. The work was slow, laborious and difficult.

The physical task of committing the dead to the earth was grim. Private John McCauley, attached to a burial party in 1918, gave a graphic account:

Often have I picked up the remains of a fine brave man on a shovel. Just a little heap of bones and maggots to be carried to the common burial place. Numerous bodies were found lying submerged in the water in shell holes and mine craters; bodies that seemed quite whole, but which became like huge masses of white, slimy chalk when we handled them. I shuddered as my hands, covered in soft flesh and slime, moved about in search of the disc, and I have had to pull bodies to pieces in order that they should not be buried unknown. It was very painful to have to bury the unknown.

Military identity tags were the most effective identification aid, intended to reveal who a serviceman was in case of severe injury, capture or death. Two fibre discs were stamped with identical details of service number, surname and initials, regiment and sometimes battalion and rank. A green tag was hung around the neck. It was accompanied by a round red tag which could be cut away, leaving the green tag on the body. Finding human remains without a red tag would indicate that the death was already in the process of being reported. Details on the green tag were also used to prepare a grave marker. Religion was referenced, so that an appropriate burial service might be provided. This could be complicated by regulations, as Reverend Crosse revealed:

Now according to the law and practice of the army a C. of E. [Church of England] chaplain had no concern with members of other denomination, and from time to time stringent orders were issued from G.H.Q. [General Headquarters] forbidding chaplains under any circumstances to bury those of other denominations than their own. In the case of R.C.'s [Roman Catholics], who deny the validity of Anglican orders, this prohibition was quite intelligible, and C. of E. chaplains, who understand this, never buried R.C.'s except by mistake. But in the case of other denominations the order was meaningless, and in most cases impracticable. Had it been observed in the letter, the only result could have been that large number of dead would have been buried without any religious ceremony.

Opposite, above: The identity discs of Private Jack Finnigan, who served in Mesopotamia during the war. The green disc was designed to stay with a man's body in the event of his death, and the red side cut off and retained by the graves registration authorities. This measure sought to ensure that bodies were reconciled with a serviceman's identity and later with his place of burial.

Opposite, below: A silver identity bracelet belonging to Rosetta Cooke, a Driver with the Women's Army Auxiliary Corps (WAAC). Cooke served in France during the war's final year where she, like other female volunteers, risked death through enemy fire, accidents or serious illness. Such bracelets ensured remains might be identified in the event of a death.

Crosse was involved in front line retrieval of soldiers' remains. He noted that the use of identity tags was not always methodical:

> It was unfortunate that well-meaning but misinformed persons often removed both identity discs at the same time without burial, a fact which explains how it was that so many unidentified dead had afterwards to be buried.

Many men also wore personal metal wrist bracelets or unofficial identity tags fashioned from coins, such was the fear of being unidentified in the event of death. Bracelets and tags were also worn by members of the women's auxiliary services, who risked their lives by volunteering overseas for work such as driving or nursing.

By 1918 587,000 graves of the British and Empire dead had been identified. There therefore remained the momentous task of locating the hundreds of thousands of people classified as 'missing'. Tell-tale signs of a body in the earth included equipment protruding from the ground, signs of vermin or discolouration of mud. Once discovered, bodies were methodically searched for army identity discs or names etched into personal possessions, from shaving mirrors to spoons. The process could often involve painstaking detective work. Reginald Bryan described the hunt for a British soldier alleged to be buried in a French village:

> On arrival there I went to the French cemetery and made an exhaustive search for a sign of the grave, but was unsuccessful. I then went into the village and asked an old man – probably the 'oldest inhabitant' – but he didn't know anything about it. I asked others and they knew nothing either; then someone remembered that a soldier did die there from an accident, but had no idea as to where he was buried. On making further enquiries I was at last successful. The village blacksmith had seen our men burying one of their 'camarades' in the village Cemetery and I went with him to the spot and he pointed out to me a little mound of earth which he said was the grave. Fortunately we knew the man's description so I was able to mark it properly and so prevent it from becoming an 'Unknown Soldiers's' grave.

'SOME CORNER OF A FOREIGN FIELD'

By 1916 the Directorate of Graves Registration and Enquiries had been established to deal with the gigantic volume of enquiries from relatives concerning grave locations. In turn, the Imperial War Graves Commission

(IWGC) was established in the following year; in 1960 it became known as the Commonwealth War Graves Commission (CWGC). A century after it was established, this organisation still records and cares for the final resting place of 1.7 million servicemen who died fighting for Britain in the First and Second World Wars, maintaining cemeteries and memorials at 23,000 locations in 153 countries.

With Fabian Ware at its head, the early IWGC was committed to an egalitarian philosophy as it planned ahead for permanent cemeteries once the war was over. It provoked some seething protests against its alleged socialist spirit, but the IWGC maintained a strident line. It issued a statement which made clear that no privilege or seniority would result in preferential treatment:

> If memorials were allowed to be erected in the War Cemeteries according to the preference, taste and means of relatives and friends, the result would be that costly monuments put by the well-to-do over their dead would contrast unkindly with those humbler ones which would be all that poorer folk could afford. Thus, the inspiring memory of the common sacrifice made by all ranks would lose the regularity and orderliness most becoming to the resting places of soldiers, who fought and fell side by side, and would, in the end, grow to be ill-assorted collections of individual monuments. Thus the governing consideration which has influenced the Commission's decision is that those who have given their lives are members of one family, and children of one mother who owes to all an equal tribute of gratitude and affection, and that, in death, all, from General to Private, of whatever race or creed, should receive equal honour under a memorial which should be the common symbol of their comradeship and of the cause for which they died.

This ethos had its roots in the collaboration between burial parties and the Graves Registration Commission's work in marking individual graves with a temporary wooden marker. The deceased's details (if they had been identified) were stamped onto a metal strip and all information recorded by Ware's unit.

When the Armistice came into effect in 1918 it became less dangerous to locate, identify and rationalise the final resting places of the British and Empire war dead. Volunteers were generally recruited from the ranks, for additional pay, to stay on the fighting fronts and undertake this work. Burying those recently killed in action and reburying some 160,000 older isolated sets of remains in new cemeteries were the priorities. The aims were set out in the House of Lords by Viscount Peel, the Under-Secretary of State for War:

A typical wooden cross of the Graves Registration Commission with an impressed aluminium name plaque in its centre. This grave marker was attributed to Sergeant H Lewis Birt, who was wounded during the Third Battle of Ypres. He died two days later and was buried in Lijssenthoek Military Cemetery. Hundreds of thousands of these crosses were erected at burial sites on the fighting fronts.

*The Cemetery, Etaples,
1919* by official war artist Sir
John Lavery. Etaples Military
Cemetery is the largest British
cemetery in France, located at
the former site of an extensive
Allied military hospital. Lavery's
painting shows women tending
to graves during the cemetery's
earliest days, before the erection
of formal headstones.

In the first place it is extremely difficult to care properly for these
scattered graves, and everyone is anxious to avoid the deplorable
experiences through which I believe this nation went some years after
the Crimean War when it was found that isolated graves – and some not
isolated – were neglected. That is one of the great reasons for doing this.
Besides, when the graves are collected in these larger cemeteries there
will be an opportunity for memorials and so on, and chapels for those
who wish to hold services for the dead, and for other arrangements which
are only possible if the dead are gathered into these larger cemeteries.

The new cemeteries were made possible by the gift of land to Britain
from the host nation (if they had been a wartime ally). The acquisition
of land in former enemy territory was settled by the Treaty of Versailles.
The bodies of former enemies were moved where possible into separate
burial grounds, where before friend and foe had lain in close proximity
out of necessity. Some of the new British cemeteries contained thousands

of bodies when a military hospital had been based nearby. Other burial grounds were established near major towns that had been embroiled in the fighting, while small, secluded cemeteries were accepted in more treacherous terrain. Reginald Bryan recalled:

> We had great difficulty in tracing the graves of British soldiers just about here as the poor fellows had been buried just where they fell, in trenches, in gun pits, on the roadside, in gardens, in fields – there were also a lot of graves of our men who died in the first part of the war in 1914.

Skeletal human remains laid out for burial at the site of a planned cemetery at Chunuk Blair in 1919. The elevated position was captured by Allied forces in August 1915, but was reclaimed by Turkish forces within days.

MEMORIALS AFTER THE WAR

The depressive psychological effects upon those engaged in the work of identifying the dead was clear. On the former Gallipoli front, Major Arthur Lees wrote in July 1919 that 'one of my section officers went to hospital with a nervous breakdown and I have one or two others on their last legs'.

Insubordination and alcohol-induced raucousness were other noted effects. There was a definite irritation at being 'left behind', as revealed in a ditty entitled *GRAVES' ELEGY IN A COMMUNAL CEMETERY* recorded in Reginald Bryan's memoir:

> *These poor young men by red tape bound*
> *Perform their tiresome daily round,*
> *While busy firms apply in vain*
> *To get them back and cry again –*
> *'Demobilize!' 'Demobilize!'*

> *There in Beaulencourt, turning grey*
> *Waiting 'allotments' day by day:*
> *They turn at last to pastures new*
> *And leave behind the G.R.U. [Graves Registration Units] –*
> *'Demoralized!' 'DEMORALIZED!'*

Reginald Bryan concluded by acknowledging the value of the mass endeavour to reconcile identities with burial places. He admitted that the task was 'somewhat depressing', but added that the men involved had derived consolation from the belief 'that it was necessary and would prove of great value and consolation to relatives of the fallen after the war'.

By 1921 some 300,000 British and Empire servicemen still remained unaccounted for. It was strongly suspected that some areas had never been searched, despite a declaration to the contrary in August 1921, and the issue was interrogated by the press and in parliament. This coincided with the depletion of available manpower. All military personnel involved in exhumation had left the former fighting fronts by October 1921, and the task of search and reburial also passed over to the IWGC. Local labourers were recruited as soldiers departed. Bodies were continually located throughout the 1920s and beyond by landowners, farmers and passers-by. Remains have occasionally been discovered in far more recent times.

As deaths mounted during the war, a hugely significant decision was taken in 1915 by the military authorities. There would be no official attempt to bring the British and Empire war dead home for burial. Nor was it permissible any longer to arrange a private repatriation. With the British and Empire deceased left near to where they had died on active service, the state now controlled the fate of their remains.

Even when families understood that repatriation was not practical in the midst of a titanic war, many were stunned – and furious – that repatriation was not made possible in peacetime. It flew in the face of many bereaved relatives' wishes. The sentiment was summed up by the Second Earl of Selborne, whose son Captain Robert Palmer was killed in action in 1916, when he declared 'these dead are not the property of the nation or of the regiment, but of the widow, of the father, and of the mother'. Yet the overwhelming majority of those who had come from Britain and across its global Empire to die in action on the Western Front, Italy, Gallipoli and Mesopotamia and beyond would never receive a funeral at home.

The ban's initial imposition was sparked in part by the fact that some wealthy families had used their plentiful means to bring the bodies of their loved ones back privately, early in the war. Lieutenant William Gladstone, killed in action in April 1915 on the Western Front, was the most prominent example. A serving MP at the time of his death and the grandson of the former prime minister of the same name, he was privately repatriated. The arrangements were made with the full consent of the War Office. Following the ban a sole concession was made for the Unknown Warrior – a single, unidentifiable British soldier who was returned to Britain and interred with great ceremony in Westminster Abbey in 1920. He had been deliberately chosen to symbolise the missing and unidentified British war dead. Many relatives found great comfort in imagining that the Unknown Warrior's anonymous remains could have been someone they were personally grieving for.

Greek labourers clear ground for a cemetery on Hill 60 on the former Gallipoli front. The cemetery was created at the site taken by New Zealand and Australian soldiers from Turkish forces until the Allies were forced to evacuate from the peninsula. The Hill 60 burial ground enlarged after the Armistice; 788 Commonwealth servicemen from the war are now buried or commemorated in this cemetery, of whom 712 are unidentified.

The repatriation of Lieutenant Gladstone led Fabian Ware (while head of his British Red Cross unit) to implore the Adjutant-General of the British Expeditionary Force, Sir Nevil McCready, to ban the private return of any further bodies in early 1915. Leaving the British and Empire dead in the countries where they had fallen was considered the best way to avoid any further disparity by way of financial means and influential connections, given the impossible logistical undertaking of sending home all human remains back to every family who desired their return. The decision also stemmed from a belief that the dead would prefer to be buried with their comrades – a much-disputed notion. Viscount Peel touched upon this in a debate in Parliament on 9 April 1919:

> Is there not some force, even some sentiment, on the other side, that it might be well, perhaps, that those who have fallen should lie together side by side in orderly array in these cemeteries – lie together in that land in which they have shed their blood and in which they have fallen?

The ban was asserted throughout the war by the army. Come peacetime, however, the fiercely emotive issue was revived once more, as responsibility

for dealing with permanent places of rest for the war dead transferred from the army to the Imperial War Graves Commission (IWCG), established by Royal Charter and accountable to the British and imperial governments that funded its work. The decision held firm in peacetime, to the astonishment of many. Its stance on the matter was clearly defined in an IWCG statement in December 1918:

> To allow removal by a few individuals (of necessity only those who could afford the cost) would be contrary to the principle of equality of treatment; to empty some 700,000 graves would be a colossal task and opposed to the spirit in which the Empire had gratefully accepted the efforts made by France, Belgium, Italy and Greece to provide land in perpetuity for our cemeteries and to adopt our dead. The Commission felt that a higher ideal than that of a private burial at home is embodied in these war cemeteries in foreign lands where those who fought and fell together, officers and men, lie together in their last resting place facing the line they gave their lives to maintain. They felt sure (and the evidence available to them confirmed the feeling) that the dead themselves, in whom the sense of comradeship was so strong, would have preferred to lie with their comrades...

The matter was debated in the House of Lords in 1919, during which the Under-Secretary of State for War, Viscount Peel, insisted:

> I deal only with the question on which I have already touched – namely, that it is only the better-to-do, the few really, who will have the opportunity or the power of removing the remains of their dead from these cemeteries to this country. And is there not some danger – I put the matter frankly before your Lordships – that if this is permitted, the millions of relatives and friends who are not in a position to make that change will feel that some invidious distinction is being set up?

This view was countered by the Marquess of Lincolnshire, on very personal grounds, with his claim that his son was the final private repatriation permitted. He protested, in the belief that poorer families would be deeply motivated to channel their limited resources to save up for a repatriation:

> My son was killed in 1915, and he was the last man brought back to England. As Lord Lieutenant of the county I have had several letters from very poor people saying, 'Oh! your son lies in Moulsoe churchyard; why cannot my husband (or my son) be brought back too?' It has been a very painful letter to have to write to say it cannot be done – that the Government cannot allow it. What Lord Selborne said is true, that amongst the poor people it is a great hardship that

their loved one is not with them. They feel that, I think, almost more than we do. And so if anything can be done, if they had a sort of consolation to think that if they could scrape money together it could be done, I am very certain in my own mind that it would be a very kind action on the part of the Government.

Instead it was hoped that if families knew precisely where their loved one had been laid to rest, and were aware of the due care that had gone into recording the location, this might provide some comfort. The IWGC was also willing to bow to family wishes and keep men in original isolated graves if relatives objected strongly to their exhumation and reburial in a new cemetery, but on the understanding that the IWGC would not maintain the grave nor facilitate the purchase of the land in perpetuity. These consolations were insufficient to stop a small number of attempted illegal exhumations. Almost every attempt was unsuccessful, with interceptions made locally or just prior to overseas travel. But a number of bodies did make it to their desired destination. This included the audacious removal of Major Charles Sutcliffe's remains from France all the way back to Canada. He had been killed in action in 1917, but Sutcliffe's remains illegally made it back to a family vault in the Ontario area.

Illegal repatriations were at the extreme end of family resistance to the decisions taken about the return of bodies. Most responses were limited to words. Gunner Harry Jervis had died from a shell wound. His mother, Ruth, was ardent in her criticism of the IWGC in one of several letters she sent to the organisation:

> Militarism has destroyed his body and it seems to me if some people in this country had the power they would deal with his soul also, but thank heaven that at least is beyond you … I think we've come to a petty state of things when a mother has to beg for the remains of her own boy. I want my boy home and I shall be satisfied with nothing less, and who has the right to deny me more under heaven?

The Jervis family was one of hundreds of thousands unable to bring their relatives home. A visit to pay respects remained out of practical reach to most families in later years. In planning permanent cemeteries on foreign soil, the IWGC forged ahead with its other major responsibility. It spearheaded an innovative approach to the design of these newly established cemeteries. Most accepted the fact of their loved one's overseas resting place. For those who did manage a visit, they would be confronted with some of the most recognisable and resonant commemorative architecture in honour of the British and Empire war dead. The IWGC's pioneering design approach became a seminal, abiding statement of remembrance.

THE UNKNOWN WARRIOR

On 11 November 1920, exactly two years after a ceasefire brought the fighting to an end, the body of the 'Unknown Warrior' was returned from the former battlefields of the Western Front and laid to rest in the Nave at Westminster Abbey. Crowds lined the streets to witness the return of this symbolically chosen, unidentified British soldier and his funeral procession was led by George V.

All but a very few families who suffered a loss during the war had been denied the traditional rites of mourning: a funeral at which they said goodbye and a nearby grave to visit their loved one. The overwhelming majority of the British and Empire dead were left in France and Belgium, and in further-flung fighting fronts such as Mesopotamia, Gallipoli and Egypt. Their graves would remain out of reach to most families. For so many there was not even a body – their lost soldier, sailor or airman would never be found, leaving anguished families with no sense of resolution. In an anonymous letter published as *To My Unknown Warrior,* an unidentified widow expressed her despair: 'I know not where they had laid him ... surely "missing" is the cruellest word in the language.'

During the war, many of the unidentified fallen had been buried beneath makeshift gravestones. David Railton, an army chaplain, was deeply affected by this sight:

I went to a billet in front of Erkingham, near Armentieres. At the back of the billet was a small garden, and in the garden, only about six paces from the house, there was a grave. At the head of the grave there stood a rough cross of white wood. On the cross was written in deep black-[p]encilled letters 'An Unknown British Soldier.'.... How that grave caused me to think!

In 1916 Railton was serving on the Western Front. Here he found himself continually concerned about the devastating effect of such uncertainty on loved ones back home.

I thought and thought and wrested in thought. What can I do to ease the pain of father, mother, brother, sister, sweetheart, wife and friend? Quietly and gradually there came out of the mist of thought this answer clear and strong, 'Let this body – this symbol of him – be carried reverently over the sea to his native land'.

Railton could not have known it then, but two more years were to pass before the Armistice was signed – time for so many more to join the ranks of the unknown dead. He conceived the idea of selecting and honouring one single unidentifiable body, symbolising all those who had died as a result of the war, and especially those who remained missing. However, he

Opposite: The coffin of the Unknown Warrior at rest in Westminster Abbey prior to his interment. During the following week an estimated 1.25 million people visited the tomb of the Unknown Warrior. A century later the site remains one of the most visited war graves in the world.

The grave of an unknown Canadian soldier on the Somme battlefield, photographed in October 1916. Leaving a dead soldier's head protection upon his grave was a common tribute after the introduction of steel helmets.

did not believe that this idea was ever likely to become 'an accomplished fact'.

After the war Railton returned to England and became vicar of St John the Baptist Church at Margate, Kent. The passing of time did nothing to alleviate his concerns. He saw how many families remained plagued by the uncertain and unknown fate of missing loved ones:

> I returned to Folkestone in 1919. Do you recall that dreadful first year of reaction? Men and nations stumbled back like badly wounded and gassed warriors to their homes. The endless shedding of blood ceased, but there was no real peace in the souls of men or nations.

Convinced that his idea of selecting a symbolic 'Unknown Warrior' and burying this body on behalf of the nation was still valid, Railton eventually wrote a letter to the Dean of Westminster, the Right Reverend Herbert Ryle, in August 1920. He outlined his idea, and his belief that the burial should take place in 'the Parish Church of the Empire'.

Railton's idea was not entirely unique. The idea that an 'unknown British hero' should be brought back from the battlefields had been given column space in the *Daily Express* in September 1919. The credit afforded to Railton as the originator of the idea was thus contested by some. Yet it was he who had written to the Dean, and it was this which set the wheels in motion to make the concept a reality.

The Dean was receptive to Railton's idea. He wrote to the king outlining the proposal, but was greeted with some reticence in a response from Lord Stamfordham, the king's private secretary, on 7 October 1920:

Nearly two years after the last shot fired on the battlefields of France and Flanders is so long ago that a funeral now might be regarded as belated, and almost, as it were, re-open war wounds, which time is generally healing.

Despite his apprehension, George V asked the Prime Minister, David Lloyd George, for his opinion on the matter. Lloyd George was in full support and the idea was subsequently approved. The Cabinet wasted little time in establishing a Memorial Service Committee tasked with organising the return and funeral service of a single unknown serviceman in a symbolic repatriation.

The success of the idea relied upon its ability to generate mass appeal, most especially with those who had suffered a bereavement where a man's death could only be officially presumed months or years later. Railton initially suggested that the symbolic dead soldier should be known as the 'unknown comrade'. The immense importance of inclusivity was understood and expressed by Lloyd George in a House of Commons debate on 1 November 1920. In it he was asked whether a sailor might be buried next to an unknown soldier so the honour might extend to both armed services:

That is a question which was very carefully considered by the cabinet, and we considered, I need hardly say, after consulting with the distinguished sailors who advise the Admiralty, and also the distinguished soldiers who advise the air board ... and the conclusion come to by all of the services was that under the circumstances the course which has been adopted is the right one. The inscription on the coffin is not 'a soldier'. He is described as an 'Unknown Warrior'. He therefore will represent all the Services.

The funeral of the 'Unknown Warrior' was planned to coincide with the second anniversary of Armistice Day on 11 November 1920. This left only a matter of weeks to make arrangements. From London the order was sent across the Channel that an unidentified body was to be selected from the former battlefields of the Western Front and returned to England. The instruction was received by Brigadier General L J Wyatt, General Officer Commanding British Troops in France and Flanders, who believed it to be a 'wonderful idea'.

With the process of exhuming and attempting to identify bodies and remains of the war dead ongoing, Wyatt would be presented with a number of men's remains; from these he was to make a random choice of one man. Contrasting details of the selection process were recorded. Wyatt's account recalled four bodies taken from each of the four big battles areas at Aisne, Somme, Arras and Ypres while Henry Williams, in his capacity with the Directorate of Graves Registration and Enquiries, remembered five bodies. Reverend George Kendall, an army chaplain, accounted for six.

Despite these divergent recollections, all of those involved agreed upon one fact: the body had to be, and was, unidentifiable. A soldier estimated to have died in a location of early fighting in the war would be most appropriate, as the progress of decomposition would make him now impossible to identify.

Lieutenant-Colonel Henry Williams was involved in the process of selecting the body:

I instructed my five officers in charge of these five different sectors which we were running that they were to produce during the next fortnight or so an unknown British soldier, with every careful attention to the fact that there could be no possible identification, and have him sent up by ambulance to my headquarters at Saint Pol in France. After the five soldiers arrived up from the five different sectors, we examined them very, very carefully to make certain there was no possible identification, even by teeth or anything else other than the fact that he was an unknown British warrior.

With officials satisfied that each was an 'unknown', the bodies were taken by Field Ambulance to headquarters at St Pol-Sur-Ternoise, 20 miles north-west of Arras. Brigadier General Wyatt confirmed the state of those from whom he was to select: 'The bodies ... were nothing but a collection of bones, placed in sacks ... each placed on a stretcher covered by a Union Jack.'

The final selection of a body was made in a chapel at St Pol by Wyatt and Lieutenant General E A S Gell of the Directorate of Graves Registration and Enquiries. The chosen remains were placed in a coffin in front of the chapel's altar where it lay until the following morning.

The coffin containing the body of the Unknown Warrior at Boulogne, on its return journey to Britain. It lay overnight in the 'chappelle ardente' within the medieval castle at Boulogne, attended by a French Guard of Honour.

Religious services were held for the dead man. From St Pol the coffin was taken to Boulogne and placed overnight under a French guard of honour.

The Unknown Warrior was placed in a casket mounted with a sixteenth-century sword taken from George V's own collection. It bore the inscription: 'A British Warrior who fell in the Great War 1914–1918 for King and Country.' With great ceremony, the coffin was loaded on board the British destroyer HMS *Verdun*, which then set sail from Boulonge bound for Dover. It was to travel onward to London by train.

At every stage of his repatriation, the Unknown Warrior was escorted by a guard of honour. Crowds flocked to catch a glimpse of his final return, pay their respects and witness the symbolic homecoming of this man who represented all of the British and Empire fallen.

On the day of the Unknown Warrior's funeral, 11 November 1920, people lined the route of his funeral procession. His coffin was drawn on a gun carriage from Victoria Station to Hyde Park Corner and onto the Mall. It then paused at Whitehall as a permanent stone memorial – the Cenotaph – was unveiled and a two minutes silence held. After receiving a wreath of roses from the king, the Unknown Warrior's coffin continued on its final journey to Westminster Abbey. *The Times* recorded the events:

The last scene in the Abbey has no parallel in history. Simplicity dominated all that was done. The coffin, borne by non-commissioned officers of the Guards, passed through the lines of a hundred wearers of the Victoria

The body of the Unknown Warrior was moved with great ceremony from the medieval castle at Boulogne on 9 November 1920. The ornate new coffin that bore him back to Britain was made of oak taken from royal land at Hampton Court near London. The coffin bore the inscription: 'A British Warrior who fell in the Great War 1914–1918 for King and Country.'

Cross. Famous men of the Forces were the pall-bearers. The King walked behind, and was followed by Princes, peers and statesmen. Choir and congregation sang the hymn 'Lead, Kindly Light'... two more hymns were sung, one of them Kipling's 'Recessional', and the service ended with the throbbing of drums and the clear call of bugles sounding the Reveille.

In life, the Unknown Warrior could have come from any social class or army rank. The funeral afforded to him, and to all those he represented, was carried out with the highest military honours. His coffin was laid to rest among royalty in the Abbey. Sir Philip Gibbs, one of several official journalists allowed access to the fighting fronts during the war, reported on the funeral:

The bringing of the Unknown Warrior from his grave in Flanders to the heart of London ... was the tribute of the nation's soul, and of all great, and humble people made equal in reverence, to the virtue of the Common Man who won the war. It was an acknowledgement before God that in the awful struggle which ended two years ago on Nov. 11 at the same hour as this soldier's halt on the way to his last resting-place in the Abbey, it was a man such as this – one of the great company of comrades, without fame, of humble rank, unknown in death – whose courage and patience, and long suffering, and obedience to the hard disciple of war saved his country in its greatest time of peril, and those who

lived at the price of his death, so that he was the Hero of that tragic epic in our history.

For many war veterans, this homecoming triggered raw memories of war and conflicting emotions: grief for the loss of comrades and guilt over their own survival. Herbert Thompson was wounded and blinded in action. In 1920 he was in the care of St Dunstan's, a charitable organisation initially established in 1915 as the Blinded Soldiers' and Sailors' Care Committee.

Thompson was chosen to attend the Unknown Warrior's funeral and was overcome by the intense experience of that day:

The ceremony in the Abbey left an indelible impression in my mind – a feeling of ineffable sadness and melancholy, yet there was a message of inspiration and hope... The atmosphere was impregnated by meaning ... clear cut pictures of France and Flanders

This panoramic shot captures the moments before the Unknown Warrior's coffin was loaded onto the Royal Navy's HMS *Verdun* at Boulogne harbour. The Unknown Warrior departed for Dover to the sound of a 19-gun salute from the escorting French flotilla and the coffin was piped on board – a tribute normally reserved for the highest ranking naval officials.

rose up before me. The dread solemnity of the occasion stirred the most poignant memories. I felt with my comrades almost ashamed that I had given so little, while he who lay sleeping by us had given all. I went away sorrowing, but with the message of hope locked in my heart.

In the week that followed an estimated 1,250,000 people visited Westminster Abbey in what the *Illustrated London News* described as the 'Mecca of the Great Pilgrimage in Memory of loved ones lost in the war'. Those who visited the grave were afforded a passing moment to remember loved ones, and all the war dead, through the prism of this one individual.

The symbolic power of the Unknown Warrior resonated deeply with the public. Some families even found comfort in the slender possibility – impossible ever to prove – that the anonymous man could be their 'missing' relative. The *Daily Express* reported on 12 November 1920:

The unending river flowed through the Abbey ... fathers and mothers, wives and sisters ... to everyone who had stood in that far straggling river of people it was 'their grave' – 'his grave'.

Soil was brought back from the Western Front for the king to scatter upon the Unknown Warrior's coffin

Top: This fragile dried rose originally formed part of one of many large commemorative wreaths that accompanied the coffin of the Unknown Warrior across the English Channel on the afternoon of 10 November 1920. The bell of HMS *Verdun* was eventually moved into Westminster Abbey as an additional tribute to the Unknown Warrior after the ship was decommissioned from service.

Above: The Unknown Warrior's arrival in England was greeted by another 19-gun salute fired from Dover Castle. After the floral wreaths were removed, military bearers carried the remains of the unknown soldier to shore to the sounds of Edward Elgar's 'Land of Hope and Glory'. The coffin was taken in a dedicated train to Victoria Station in London, where it remained overnight.

during its interment. The following year, on the third anniversary of the Armistice in 1921, the temporary stone placed on top of his grave was replaced by a permanent Belgian marble plinth. It was inscribed with words written by the Dean of Westminster:

> BENEATH THIS STONE RESTS THE BODY
> OF A BRITISH WARRIOR
> UNKNOWN BY NAME OR RANK
> BROUGHT FROM FRANCE TO LIE AMONG
> THE MOST ILLUSTRIOUS OF THE LAND
> AND BURIED HERE ON ARMISTICE DAY
> 11 NOV: 1920, IN THE PRESENCE OF
> HIS MAJESTY KING GEORGE V
> HIS MINISTERS OF STATE
> THE CHIEFS OF HIS FORCES
> AND A VAST CONCOURSE OF THE NATION
> THUS ARE COMMEMORATED THE MANY
> MULTITUDES WHO DURING THE GREAT
> WAR OF 1914– 1918 GAVE THE MOST THAT
> MAN CAN GIVE LIFE ITSELF
> FOR GOD
> FOR KING AND COUNTRY
> FOR LOVED ONES HOME AND EMPIRE
> FOR THE SACRED CAUSE OF JUSTICE AND
> THE FREEDOM OF THE WORLD
> THEY BURIED HIM AMONG THE KINGS
> BECAUSE HE
> HAD DONE GOOD TOWARD GOD AND
> TOWARD
> HIS HOUSE

The Unknown Warrior's body and burial were intended to be tangible comforts for grief-stricken families. The idea was replicated by other nations, namely France's Unknown Soldier, laid to rest at the base of the Arc de Triomphe in Paris in 1921. In London, the Unknown Warrior's homecoming had not opened old wounds, as the king had feared; instead it went some way towards healing them. The anonymous widow, in her letter *To My Unknown Warrior,* felt some consolation:

> I shall never again have to read those cruel words 'Regret – No trace'... I have found you at last. To-day the heart's longing of her waiting years has been fulfilled and your mother is content because she has stood beside the place of your rest, because you are lonely and lost no more.

The coffin's entrance to Westminster Abbey, followed by George V, at the funeral of the Unknown Warrior in London on 11 November 1920. Dozens of war widows were invited to attend the funeral service along with military, political and religious leaders.

The war had deprived hundreds of thousands of families of the chance to mourn a lost loved one formally at a local place of rest that they could visit. While other memorials recognised death on a mass scale and paid tribute to those whose remains were never recovered, the Unknown Warrior literally embodied this loss. His symbolic funeral and burial at 'home' gave some comfort to grieving British families. But the commemoration of those whose remains were left abroad was to pose a prodigious challenge.

EMMA HARROLD
Curator

4

THEIR NAME LIVETH
FOR EVERMORE

Establishing permanent burial grounds for British and Empire soldiers, and maintaining a formal record of each grave, was not simply an administrative and logistical marathon. Dignified commemoration at these resting places was also a core responsibility of the Imperial War Graves Commission (IWGC). Fabian Ware – pioneer of the process of recording where Britain's war dead were buried during the war – was once again at the helm. Under his leadership as the IWGC's Vice-President, an extraordinary approach to honouring the war dead was established through design principles for permanent cemeteries and memorials.

Following months of debate and impasse, Ware asked Sir Frederic Kenyon to interpret and draw conclusions from contrasting architectural ideas and proposals for British and Empire burial grounds. The ground-breaking report that Kenyon, Director of the British Museum, presented to the Commission in 1918 emphasised equality as its core creed; it also sought to avoid an overly religious or victorious tone. His conclusions were presented under the heading 'WAR GRAVES: HOW THE CEMETERIES ABROAD WILL BE DESIGNED'. This highly sensitive mission was introduced and contextualised in the report's early pages by Fabian Ware, acutely aware of the morass of conflicting attitudes:

> The Commission recognised that there would inevitably be considerable difference of opinion on the question of how the Cemeteries abroad should be laid out, and what form of permanent memorial should be erected in them. They felt, moreover, that it was undesirable that a matter of this kind should become the subject of controversy, if it could be avoided.

DESIGNS FOR RESTING PLACES

Sir Frederic Kenyon made visits to existing cemeteries as part of his research, as he took into account military, bereaved, religious and artistic viewpoints. He drew upon landscaping expertise from the Royal Botanic Gardens at Kew, and took literary advice from the prominent poet and author Rudyard Kipling. As a result of Kenyon's preferences, three of Britain's most eminent architects – Sir Edwin Lutyens, Sir Herbert Baker and Sir Reginald Blomfield – were subsequently appointed to further develop guiding principles. Each individual cemetery and memorial to the missing could then be built according to the trio's guidelines. One abiding principle was inarguable: 'The Commissioners are of the opinion that no distinction should be made between officers and men lying in the same cemeteries in the form or nature of the memorials.'

Kenyon made clear the sensitivity of his recommendations and the considerations he had borne in mind in his report:

Opposite: Sir Frederic George Kenyon (1863–1952). His 1918 report on the design of burial grounds for British and Empire war dead proved a seminal document, with hundreds of permanent cemeteries and memorials to the missing laid out in accordance with its recommendations.

Previous page: The imposing Ypres (Menin Gate) Memorial, completed in 1927. Inscribed on the arch are the names of over 54,000 British and Empire soldiers who died before 16 August 1917 in the area around the town of Ypres. None have a known grave.

My endeavour has been to arrive at a result which will, so far as may be, satisfy the feelings of relatives and comrades of those who lie in these cemeteries; which will represent the soldierly spirit and discipline in which they fought and fell; which will typify the Army to which they belonged; which will give expression to those deeper emotions, of regimental comradeship, of service to their Army, their King, their Country and their God, which underlay (perhaps often unconsciously) their sacrifice of themselves for the cause in which they fought, and which in ages to come will be a dignified memorial, worthy of the nation and of the men who gave their lives for it, in the lands of the Allies with whom and for whom they fought.

The ethos of the military and the attitudes of bereaved families were key concerns. So was giving equal consideration to the hundreds of thousands of 'missing' soldiers who had disappeared without trace.

And while dealing with this part of the subject [the diversity of cemetery sites], it may be as well to remind some who may read this report that of many who have fallen in this war there can be no identified grave. Many bodies are found but cannot be identified; many are never found at all; many are buried in graves which have subsequently been destroyed in the course of fighting. This is especially the case in areas such as that of Ypres, where the same ground has been contested for three consecutive years, and the whole countryside has been blasted and torn with shell fire. Therefore, whatever may be done in the way of placing individual monuments over the dead, in very many cases no such monument is possible. Yet these must not be neglected, and some memorial there must be to the lost, the unknown, but not forgotten dead.

Kenyon's report laid bare the starkest fact about First World War remembrance: – that by deciding not to bring the British and Empire war dead back home, mourning those who died abroad on active service could not be accompanied by funerals attended by families or visits to a local graveside.

It is necessary to face the fact that this decision has given pain in some quarters, and pain which the Commissioners would have been glad to avoid. Not a few relatives have been looking forward to placing a memorial of their own choosing over the graves which mean so much to them; some have devoted much time and thought to making such a memorial beautiful and significant. Yet it is hoped that even these will realize that they are asked to join in an action of even higher significance. The sacrifice of the individual is a great idea and worthy of commemoration; but the community of sacrifice, the service of a common cause, the comradeship of arms which has brought together men of all ranks and grades – these are greater ideas, which should be commemorated in those cemeteries where they lie together, the representatives of their country in the lands in which they served.

The design principles for the cemeteries were finalised following the construction of three representative cemeteries in France, to assess the financial viability of proposed design features. Amendments were made accordingly. Kenyon also believed it was vital that burial grounds' functions as cemeteries 'should be evident at first sight, and should be constantly present to the minds of those who pass by or who visit them'. Consistency was key to his vision, including the use of walls to mark boundaries and the provision of access to a printed register of those buried in each cemetery. It further extended to horticultural considerations, with durability another factor. Drawing on expert guidance and recommendations from Kew's Royal Botanical Gardens, Kenyon laid out the anticipated effects:

> There is no reason why cemeteries should be places of gloom; but the restfulness of grass and the brightness of flowers in fitting combination would appear to strike the proper note of brightness and life. Care must be taken that the grass is properly mown, and that the flowers do not grow in such profusion as to overshadow the headstones and disguise the fact that the place is a cemetery.

HEADSTONES FOR HEROES

The most intimate aspect of the IWGC's work centred on headstone designs for individual graves. Kenyon was strongly in favour a stone of exactly the same dimensions for every person, where possible. What was more, 'ordered ranks' of headstones would help to give 'the appearance as of a battalion on parade, and suggesting the spirit of discipline and order which is the soul of an army'. Most of all, Kenyon believed, individual headstones could provide consolation to bereaved families:

> Many of them, as indicated above, will be disappointed that they are not allowed to erect their own monument over their own dead; but they will be much more disappointed if no monument except a mere indication number marks that grave at all. The individual headstone, marking the individual grave, will serve as centre and focus of the emotions of the relatives who visit it.

Left: A stonemason from the Imperial War Graves Commission at work. The headstone he is shown engraving was that of Private John Christopher Weatherhead of the Canadian Army Medical Corps at Doullens Communal Cemetery in France.

Overleaf: A selection of designs for British Army regimental badges for use on headstones in Imperial War Graves Commission cemeteries. The designs were created to facilitate straightforward hand engraving.

A rounded-top design was considered to be universally appropriate for all servicemen. Yet differences between men were incorporated, as revealed in original headstone schedules for every grave. Religious belief was acknowledged in final designs, with the majority of stones inscribed with a simple Christian cross or an alternative symbol such as the Jewish 'Star of David'. Military decorations were also taken into account in written inscriptions. In the case of the Victoria Cross, given in recognition of conspicuous gallantry in the face of the enemy, and the highest award in the British honours system, the outline shape of the award featured prominently on the headstone. In areas where the terrain was unstable, flat headstones were used. Occasionally different types of stone local to an area were utilised, otherwise the majority of headstones were a strictly consistent shape. White Portland stone from Dorset was chosen as the principal material in the mass production of permanent new headstones. Durability was the key consideration to ensure low-cost upkeep: these cemeteries were built to last. The standardised, rounded-top shape of the stone and its precise dimensions of 76 cm (30 inches) tall, 38 cm (15 inches) wide and 7.6 cm (3 inches) thick caused consternation to some, as expressed in the House of Lords by Lord Balfour of Burleigh in 1919:

> But the question I want to raise is why it is necessary that the headstones should be absolutely uniform. Why should it be in a form which will look like nothing else but a line of milestones? That seems to be a wholly inadequate memorial of the sacrifices which have been made and the feelings of those who are left behind.

The Earl of Selborne was even more forceful, claiming that it was 'nothing less than sheer tyranny – a gross and wicked tyranny' to impose a headstone design and 'state that a cross may not be substituted for one of these tombstones if that is the wish of the widow, of the father, or of the mother'. Despite such resistance, this was a principle on which those conceiving the cemeteries' design refused to be moved.

Frederic Kenyon's steer towards – and Fabian Ware's commitment to – design uniformity were also underpinned by an aversion to the 'jumbled mass' of civilian headstone tributes in cemeteries on the Western Front that were 'neither dignified nor inspiring'. The Under-Secretary of State for War, Viscount Peel, outlined in London on 9 April 1919 how the design language for each headstone had developed:

> Perhaps I may detail to my noble friend what is the general design: a tombstone with the regimental badge at the top, and below the name and number of the man, and again below that an incised cross, and

Nº 1030/2   LANCASHIRE FUSILIE

TOP LINE OF INSCRIPTION

Nº 1031/1   EAST LANCASHIRE REGIMENT

TOP LINE OF INSCRIPTION

Nº 1029/1   KING'S ROYAL RIFLE CORPS

TOP LINE OF INSCRIPTION

Nº 1033/1   SOUTH LANCASHIRE REGT

TOP LINE OF INSCRIPTION   7/8"

Nº 1074/1   ROYAL LANCASTER REGIMENT

TOP LINE OF INSCRIPTION   7/8"

Nº 1036/1   LEINSTER REGIMENT   MacD

TOP LINE OF INSCRIPTION   7/8"

Nº 1035/1   LEICESTERSHIRE REGIMENT

TOP LINE OF INSCRIPTION   7/8"

Nº 1038/1   THE KING'S LIVERPOOL REGIMENT   M

below again an inscription. The inscription is left almost entirely to the suggestion of the relatives of the dead men. Of course, there must be some limitation as to the length and nature of that inscription, but, broadly speaking, suggestions are invited from the relatives, and those suggestions are fully carried out.

Standardised lettering for the inscriptions on headstones and memorials was created by graphic designer, letterer and architect Macdonald Gill. He also designed regimental badge outlines – a diverse array of designs that Kenyon hoped would 'gratify the regimental feeling which is so strong a characteristic of the British Army'. Personal text inscriptions at the foot of each headstone were also permitted but were strictly controlled; they were limited to approximately three lines and 'of the nature of a text or prayer'. There was a charge for this addition, effectively preventing families without spare funds the opportunity for personalisation, supervised as it was. The IWGC had the final say on each and every inscription, with Ware being wary that it 'is clearly undesirable to allow free scope for the effusions of the mortuary mason, the sentimental versifier, or the crank'.

Requests to push the bounds of these guidelines and individualise a person's grave more prominently were repeatedly rebuffed by the IWGC. In 1927 the family of war poet Private Isaac Rosenberg failed in their attempt to honour his artistic talents in the main portion of the headstone, following the discovery of his remains the year before:

> With reference to the form which you have returned, I am to express regret that the Commission are unable to accede to your request to engrave the words 'Artist and Poet' after the name of Private I. Rosenberg in the Military inscription on the headstone that is to be erected over his grave.
>
> I am however, to say that they could be engraved at the foot of the stone as the personal inscription at your expense.

The government of New Zealand took umbrage with the decision to charge for personal inscriptions, instead imposing a blanket ban on personal tributes for its dead servicemen. Despite feeling the wrath of some of its bereaved citizens, prominent New Zealand politician Sir James Allen, who had himself lost a son on the Gallipoli front, reflected the government's position in 1924:

> Had we allowed personal inscriptions on the headstones, we should have had all the rich people making use of the privilege and the poor would

The Imperial War Graves cemetery at Louvencourt, on the former Somme battlefields. There are now 151 Commonwealth burials in this cemetery, with interred soldiers' deaths dating from 1915 to 1918. The cemetery was one of three 'model' burial grounds laid out after the First World War. These tester cemeteries trialled design features that were ultimately rolled out across all Imperial War Graves Commission cemeteries.

> not have been able to, a distinction we had no desire to encourage ... So far as New Zealand is concerned, we have definitely decided not to permit personal inscriptions, and we are going to stick to it.

When the headstones became a reality, the original temporary wooden crosses which had served as grave markers were shipped home upon request. They were sometimes incorporated into memorials, acquiring the status of near-relics.

CEMETERY MONUMENTS

The simple religious inscriptions made to headstones did not satisfy all demands for overt Christian symbolism in military burial grounds. Although these calls were robustly countered, a compromise was eventually reached. Every large cemetery was tasked with incorporating two central structures: a secular Stone of Remembrance and a Christian-inspired Cross of Sacrifice. Kenyon considered the function of a central monument in his report:

> It is essential that it should be simple, durable, dignified and expressive of the higher feelings with which we regard our dead. In order to do

this, it must have, or be capable of, religious associations, and while it must satisfy the religious emotions of as many as possible, it must give no reasonable ground of offence to any. The central sentiment of our commemoration of the dead is, I think, a grateful and undying remembrance of their sacrifice, and it is this sentiment which most persons will wish to see symbolised in the central monument.

The Stone of Remembrance was designed by Sir Edwin Lutyens. An altar 12 feet (3.6 m) in length, raised upon steps, the Stone was trialled in the three model cemeteries. It was thereafter decided that the Stone would be incorporated into larger cemeteries. Frederic Kenyon expressed concern about the impact of the elements, as 'a dripping stone, covered with fallen leaves or bird-droppings, has a forlorn and dreary aspect'. But the idea was embraced. Although Lutyens was determined to keep his design as secular as possible, Kenyon proposed that the Stone ought to bear 'some fine thought or words of sacred dedication':

I would only suggest that it must be short, and that its effectiveness must not depend upon literary associations, which do not exist for the majority of those who will read it. A phrase from the Bible, or some words which will of themselves strike the right note in the hearts of those who read them, is what is required.

Stonemasons engrave Chinese characters into Imperial War Graves Commission headstones to record the details of deceased members of the Chinese Labour Corps. The Imperial War Graves Commission cared for the graves of Chinese labourers who had been recruited to assist British forces and had died during their service.

That task was passed on to Rudyard Kipling. The renowned poet and writer was also a bereaved father; his only son, John, had been killed at the Battle of Loos in 1915. In Kipling's lifetime his son's body was never found. He spent four years painstakingly trying to uncover further details about John's fate, but by 1919 came to accept that his son – officially declared 'missing' – must have been killed at Loos, aged 18. Decades later, in the 1990s, a previously unidentified soldier was deemed by the Commonwealth War Graves Commission to be John Kipling. His father had been responsible for the phrase 'Lest We Forget', a line in his famous 1897 poem, 'Recessional'. The words were adopted as a well-worn warning in the aftermath of the First World War. In his work with the IWGC, Kipling recommended 'Their name liveth for evermore' for the Stone of Remembrance, a biblical text from the Book of Ecclesiasticus. He also penned a simple tribute for the headstones of the unidentified: 'A soldier of the Great War. Known unto God.' This phrase dealt neatly with the fact that so many bodies, or parts of bodies, were in a pitiful state upon discovery, and thus unable to be identified.

The second major cemetery monument, the Cross of Sacrifice, was designed by Sir Reginald Blomfield. His concept was determinedly simple but starkly Christian. Kenyon was adamant that the inclusion of a cross was appropriate, declaring 'I have no doubt that great distress would be felt if our cemeteries lacked this recognition of the fact that we are a Christian Empire, and this symbol of the self-sacrifice made by those who lie in them'.

However, Britain's global Empire forces were religiously diverse, a fact that was duly outlined in Kenyon's report:

> One large and important class must be dealt with separately. It will be understood that where our Mohammedan, Hindu, and other non-Christian fellow subjects lie (and care has always been taken to bury them apart) their graves will be treated in accordance with their own religious beliefs and practices, and their own religious symbol will be placed over them. On this point it is essential that the Commission should be guided by the advice of those who are most conversant with our Indian and African Empires.
>
> The religious requirements of the different castes and creeds must be scrupulously respected, and the designs of mosques or temples erected in Moslem and Hindu cemeteries should be in conformity with the religious customs and aspirations of the particular creed concerned. The Commission will no doubt desire that no less honour should be paid to the last resting places of Indian and other non-Christian members of the Empire than to those of our British soldiers.

The Kenyon report was a seminal document. The IWGC accepted his recommendations for the future on 18 February 1918, as the war was still

raging. In peacetime a flurry of construction resulted in the creation of more than 500 permanent cemeteries and 400,000 headstones by 1927. This included the graves of many men who had died back in Britain. Thousands died from wounds or illness on the home front, having been transferred back to British hospitals for treatment. They were granted IWGC headstones, either in military sections of larger cemeteries or mixed in among civilian gravestones in smaller churchyards. Brookwood Cemetery in Surrey was the largest burial ground in the world when it opened in 1854. Land was set aside there in 1917 for the burial of servicemen and women who had been transported home and had died in the London Military District. This included men from Empire countries including Australia, the British West Indies, Canada, India, Newfoundland, New Zealand and South Africa.

MEMORIALS FOR THE MISSING

The stark fact remains to this day that hundreds of thousands of British and Empire soldiers were never located or identified, and never formally buried. They were blown to unrecognisable pieces, entombed by mud or drowned at sea. Memorials to the missing were therefore just as important a concern as the decisions over burial and graves.

Battles had been fought at or near the Belgian town of Ypres in 1914, 1915, 1917 and 1918. The area had been at the scene of continuous fighting for years. After Winston Churchill's suggestion that the ruins of Ypres should be preserved as a 'sacred place' were ignored, the IWGC settled upon the design for a great arch – to be situated symbolically, with the agreement of Belgian authorities, where thousands of troops had marched in and out of the town. Sir Reginald Blomfield's Ypres (Menin Gate) Memorial was inscribed with the names of over 54,000 British and Empire soldiers who had died in the area but were never afforded a known place of burial.

Sir Edwin Lutyens' even more imposing memorial at Thiepval on the former Western Front is the largest British Empire or Commonwealth war memorial in the world. It commemorates more than 72,000 men of British and South African forces who died in the area before 20 March 1918. None have a known grave and most died during the Battle of the Somme in 1916. At 45 metres (nearly 150 feet) high, Lutyens' design was titanic in scale, reflecting the huge number of missing men whom it commemorated. Construction of the immense tribute began in 1928 and took four years to build, slowed by the discovery of unexploded ordnance on this former battlefield. Since its completion, names have been removed when a man's remains were later discovered and identified. The memorial is still a staggering reminder of the war's ability to eradicate any trace of a person.

Losses at sea posed particular problems. Wherever naval, hospital, merchant and transport ships were sunk, bodies simply disappeared without trace. Over 600 men – primarily South African labourers – lost their lives in the English Channel after SS *Mendi* was accidentally struck in fog by another ship on 21 February 1917. A small number of bodies eventually washed up along the South Coast, most of them near Portsmouth. These men were buried in nearby graveyards and later received IWGC headstones. The ship's wreck remained undiscovered until 1974, and a further three decades were to pass before the Ministry of Defence was able to designate the wreck a war grave under the Protection of Military Remains Act 1986. The loss of life in this disaster was eventually commemorated on a number of memorials, such as the Mendi Memorial at Avalon Cemetery in Soweto, South Africa, which was unveiled in 1995.

The missing dead from SS *Mendi* were commemorated on a memorial at Hollybrook Cemetery in Southampton, as were 1,900 servicemen and women who were lost at sea during the war as a result of German U-boat action, mines or accidents. Among their number was Lord Kitchener, the Secretary of State for War and the figurehead of British Army recruitment. He drowned in 1916 off the coast of the Orkney Islands, where he was en route to allied Russia. The shockwaves of his death were felt throughout the Empire, where he was a household name. His body was never found, a fact which gave rise to wild conspiracy theories about his fate.

A scale drawing of the west elevation of the Thiepval Memorial to the Missing. It commemorates more than 72,000 men of British and South African forces who died in the Somme area before the start of the German spring offensive in 1918. They have no known grave, and most were presumed dead in the Battle of the Somme in 1916.

Whether human remains were found or lost forever, the IWGC's egalitarian principles reflected a transformative attitude in the treatment of the majority of the British and Empire war dead. This vision was clear to see in headstone, cemetery and memorial designs. No longer were the rank and file perceived as one of society's lowest common denominators, as the much maligned professional soldier had been viewed in the nineteenth century. Now, whether interred or commemorated by a simple inscription, men and their officers were equals in death; they were treated as individuals in this fusion of imperial and individual remembrance, even when their remains could not be identified. They were part of a revolutionary democracy of death. The financial commitment to the maintenance of graves, cemeteries

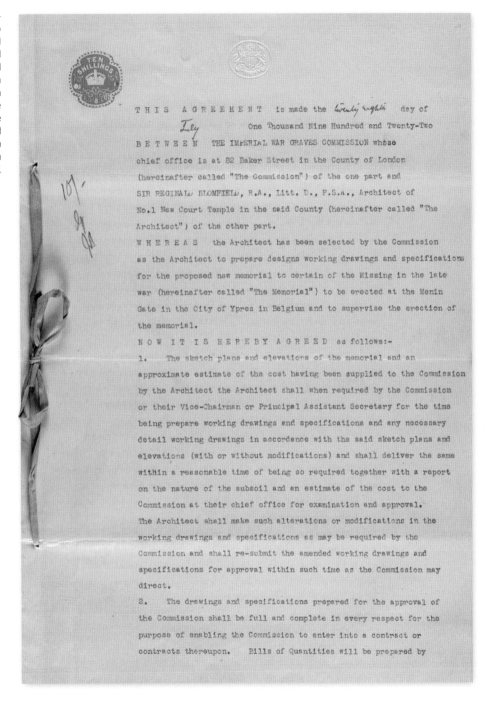

A page of the contract drawn up in 1922 between the Imperial War Graves Commission and architect Sir Reginald Blomfield to design the Ypres (Menin Gate) Memorial to the missing in the Belgian town of Ypres. The memorial arch was built over the spot where troops had marched into the town and out to battle in actions over the four years, from which so many never returned.

and memorials has endured to this day, expanding as new conflicts involving British forces have wrought more violence and caused further deaths. The endeavour behind the cemeteries and their designs was enormous. Yet such efforts were rarely sufficient succour for families struggling with losses that cut far deeper than a stone inscription.

5

REMEMBERING AT HOME

When faced with a bereavement, with no solace to be found in a funeral or a nearby grave, families and friends of those who had died serving abroad were forced to apply creative zeal to their commemorative efforts. People found ways in which to keep the memory of their loved one alive. The simplest items could become treasured relics, while elaborate memorials were made possible by wealth and influence.

A modest cluster of Private Albert Tattersall's effects were returned to his father in November 1916, four months after his death from wounds in France while serving with the Manchester regiment. An official list advised of the return of one disc, one wallet, a packet of letters, photos and cards, as well as one pipe, one coin, one pouch, one pair of scissors, one jack knife, two prayer books and one bag. Such ordinary possessions became a consoling connection with a lost relative, conjuring up the rituals of his daily life and the small pleasures enjoyed in his last days.

Lieutenant Stewart Montagu Cleeve of the Royal Garrison Artillery made a special effort to return an item of religious comfort he discovered on the Somme sector to a casualty's home:

> I came across a sergeant lying dead on the ground with his hand on an open bible. It was a Douai [*sic*] Bible, and from that I knew he was a Catholic.

Above left: A photograph of the three Tattersall brothers, with Private Albert Tattersall shown bottom right. His two brothers were also serving soldiers in the 20th Battalion Manchester Regiment, a battalion unit known as the 5th City 'Pals'.

Previous page: Private William 'Will' Martin of the Devonshire Regiment and his fiancée Emily Chitticks. Will was a farm hand from Cornwall who enlisted in 1914, shortly after the outbreak of war. He met Emily while stationed in Essex for his military training and the pair had a whirlwind romance. An abundance of letters sent between the couple survive as a testament to their lost love following Will's death on active service in 1917.

The shrapnel was pouring over our heads, but I closed his eyes, then closed the book and put it in my pocket before crawling back to the front line. Later on I took his address from it and sent it home to his widow.

KEEPING MEMORIES ALIVE

During the war the Army Postal Service's London depot administered every item of mail sent by families to their loved ones on the Western Front. The five-acre site handled an astonishing two billion letters and 114 million parcels during the conflict. In return, letters and postcards were received at home as prized proofs of life. After a death, they became delicate treasures that captured a dead person's affection, humour and sometimes their grumbles. The potential for death hung constantly over relationships between those on the home and fighting fronts. As such, the warmth and love conveyed in many letters was often palpably and generously expressed.

A poignant collection of 78 letters and postcards was kept by Emily Chitticks, the fiancée of William ('Will') Martin. The letters reveal a passionate bond between the couple, who became engaged during the war. Will was a farm hand from Cornwall. Having enlisted in 1914, shortly

good riddance for there is
nothing but rows & deceitfulness
going on where he is. Well
darling I dont know much
more to say now, so will close
with fondest love & kisses from
Your Loving Little Girl

xxxxx Emily xxx
xxxx

P.S. Cheer up darling, & dont worry
about me I am quite alright,
only anxious to get your letters
there is good news in the paper
Love from Mum & Dad.

Suffolk House
Herongate
Brentwood
Essex

28/3/17.

My Dearest Will. I feel I must
write you again dear altho there
is not much news to tell you.
I wonder how you are getting on,
I shall be so relieved to get a letter
from you, I cant help feeling a
bit anxious dear. I know how
you must have felt darling when
you did not get my letters for
so long. Of course I know dear
you will write as soon as ever
you can but the time seems so
dull & weary without any news
of you if only this war was
over dear, & we were together
again It will be one day. I

Left: An envelope addressed by Emily Chitticks to her finance Will Martin, containing a letter that he never received. Both were returned, the envelope emblazoned with the stark official reference: 'KILLED'.

Below left: A letter sent by Emily Chitticks to her 'Dearest Will', dated one day after his death in 1917. In it she expresses concern that he had not written to her for some time: 'I feel I must write you again dear altho' there is not much news to tell you. I wonder how you are getting on. I shall be so relieved to get a letter from you. I can't help feeling a bit anxious dear.'

after the outbreak of war, he met Emily while based in her home county of Essex. Will was stationed there during his military training and a whirlwind romance ensued. After he was sent to the Western Front, the couple regularly corresponded. But in early 1917 Emily expressed acute unease when Will failed to respond to her letters. The reality, as she feared, was that he was already dead, killed by a sniper's bullet. Several months later, although it never came to be, Emily expressed a fervent hope for Will's correspondence 'to be buried with me, as my heart & love are buried in his grave in France'. Emily's letters were eventually deposited in the archives of the Imperial War Museum instead, given the historical significance of the originals in revealing the grave impact of the war upon relationships. Copies of the letters were buried with Emily when she died in 1974, having never married.

Emily and Will's story speaks to the devastation felt by many of the bereaved, and its lifelong impact. Paper messages sent during the war were retained for decades by many grief-stricken partners. Handwritten letters scribbled to and from the home front stirred up the powerful language of lost love.

When news of a death was received, photographs became cherished mantelpiece memorials in homes across the country. During and after the First World War there were few families without some kind of scratchy sepia snapshot of husbands, sons and brothers in uniform. Smiles and serious stares captured in photographs were immortalised as fragile family heirlooms. These images were often framed alongside posthumously issued medals.

Photographs of individuals were also sometimes reproduced in local newspaper obituaries. Years before the advent of the domestic 'wireless', and decades before the invention of television, newspapers were the primary source of information. As well as more lengthy obituaries, printed casualty lists delivered the shock news to anxious acquaintances who scoured them. In 1917 a national shortage of paper stopped the inclusion of casualty lists in national newspapers. They continued to be published weekly by the government, but had to be purchased at a cost of three pence each.

Memorial booklets and cards were compiled by families in scrapbook fashion to convey grief and loving pride in the life lost. Some were unique items kept at home; others were published. Captain Charles Aubrey Town of the 'Leeds Pals', 11th Battalion West Yorkshire Regiment, was eulogised in one such booklet after he was killed in action in Belgium on 20 September 1917. Distributed within his local community, it was crammed with photographs and shared memories of his achievements. Brimming with tributes from fellow officers from their original letters of condolence, these included the sorrows of an unnamed major:

Notes.

August: 9th 1916. The Day I first met
"Will."

October 24th. "Engaged to Will."
Nov: early Will went to Holt.
from there to Devonport.
Last week in Nov: Will came up
on his last leave. spent at
Southend. Dec: 4th left Devonport
for Southampton. Dec: 6th Sailed
for France. March 27th Will
fell asleep. Killed in Action.
April 6. Received this terrible
blow. May & June, Letters
to Will returned. May. I
received his Will. All love &
cherished
hopesgone now, buried in a
grave with my darling boy
"somewhere in France".
Hope to meet him again in Heaven
The End. in this life. & the
Beginning in the next, Amen.

June 6th 1917

Sacred to the memory of my.
Darling Sweetheart Will. The
only boy I love with my whole
heart & soul, who loved me so
well he gave his all, his life
for me. When I die. I wish
all his letters to be buried
with me, as my heart & love
are buried in his grave in France
Parted on this   (Emily Ellen Chitticks)
earth to be united
the next   (William James Martin.)

His loss is felt by everyone in the battalion, from the Colonel down to the most recently joined private. There was no more popular officer in the battalion than he, none more gallant. He was conscientious and thorough in all he did, and looked after his men like a father. I saw him at 4.30am, when he was just preparing to get his men into their assembly positions. He was, as usual, perfectly cool and self-possessed, and was going about his work as though the enemy was 100 miles away instead of 100 yards. It was this quality of his which gave his men such confidence.

Jessie Nicholson, widow of Lance Corporal Ernest Nicholson, had several memorial cards produced in tribute to her husband. One version was signed off by 'his broken-hearted Wife and little Son Clifford', while another featured the consoling words of a poem:

Emily Chitticks never married following the death of her fiancé Will Martin in 1917. She survived him by many decades, dying in 1974. Emily was adamant that she wanted to be buried with Will's letters. Their correspondence was deemed of such significance that the originals were given to the archives of the Imperial War Museum as a memento of their love cut short, while copies were buried with Emily following her death.

A memorial silk from 1917. It was commissioned in memory of Private Joseph Bowker by his 'sorrowing' family in Lancashire.

At night when the stars are shining,
Over a silent grave,
There lies our dear one sleeping,
Whose memory will never fade.

Memorial 'silks' were a more unusual method of remembering an individual. Not entirely novel to the First World War, these bookmark-style mementoes were distributed among family and friends – possibly with the intent of placing the silk into the pages of a Bible. The family of Private Joseph Bowker included a small circular photograph on their tasselled memorial silk, along with the words:

HE NOBLY DID HIS DUTY, In Loving Memory of Private Joseph Bowker, No. 19154, Border Regiment, aged 25 years; Who Died of Wounds August 10th, 1917, received in action in France in the great European War. It's only a mother who knows the sorrow, It's only a mother who knows the pain, Of losing a son she loved so dearly, and to know she cannot see him again. From his sorrowing MOTHER, SISTERS and BROTHERS. 145 Glebe Street, Leigh, Lancashire

A photograph of a munitions worker whose left forearm was tattooed with the name of her sweetheart who had died on active service. She later had a memorial cross added to this very personal form of tribute.

Another unusual but enduring tribute came in the form of memorial tattoos. Names and symbols, from crosses to flowers, were painfully applied to the skin as an indelible reminder of someone dear.

Babies too sometimes became a striking form of 'living' remembrance. The battles in which their fathers had fought, and sometimes died, were appropriated as names for some of the nation's newest citizens. During the war years 1,634 children born in Britain were given eye-catching names inspired by the conflict. Place names of major actions provided the most compelling inspiration. Verdun, although not a British action, was the most popular, with 901 wartime babies named after this bloody clash led by French forces. The locations of British battles were also commemorated, with 71 children named after Ypres and 58 after Mons. Feminine variants such as Dardenella and Sommeria were applied to baby girls, commemorating the Dardanelles naval campaign of 1915 and the 1916 Battle of the Somme respectively. Even German bombing raids on British towns by 'Zeppelin'-type airships might be commemorated, as in the naming of little Zeppelina Clark in Essex, born on the night of a dramatic raid. Clearly naming babies to remember the war was a niche trend. Yet even today a small number of baby names continue to be inspired by the conflict, passed down through families in memory of a relative's war service.

MEMORIALS, MEDALS AND PLAQUES

Stained-glass memorials could provide powerful tributes to those who died in the First World War. Commissioning an artist to design an elaborate stained-glass window in tribute to a single serviceman was only the preserve of a wealthy, well-connected few. Second Lieutenant Isaac Althorp Ridgway, for instance, died in May 1915 while serving with Australian forces in Gallipoli. His face was incorporated into a colourful window on the top of a figure wearing medieval knight's armour in St Peter's Church in Oughtrington, Cheshire, close to his parents' home in England.

Figures who had dominated public life were also part of the war's tragic roll call. Shock and disbelief greeted the death of Lord Kitchener, presumed drowned after the sinking of HMS *Hampshire* in 1916. As the serving

MURDERED

OCTOBER 12TH, 1915

By THE Huns

MISS EDITH CAVELL

ENLIST IN THE 99th

AND HELP STOP SUCH ATROCITIES

PUBLISHED BY THE ESSEX COUNTY RECRUITING COMMITTEE

8

Record Print, Windsor

Secretary of State for War, hailed as a heroic leader of late nineteenth-century imperial campaigns in Africa, Kitchener had been adored by the public. His life and death were commemorated in the same way that this 'face' of the British war effort had been celebrated during his lifetime – by a torrent of commercially produced ephemera.

The war precipitated ordinary people to dramatic fame as a result of their perceived martyrdom. The British nurse Edith Cavell was executed by the Germans on 12 October 1915 in Brussels for the war crime of helping Allied military prisoners to escape. She had been in the German-occupied city to set up a nurses' training school. Her death was harnessed in strident recruitment propaganda that sought to outrage men across the British Empire into becoming soldiers to avenge her. In tribute to the nurse, 25 British baby girls were given the name Cavell during the war.

Some of those who performed courageous individual actions on the fighting fronts also became celebrated as heroes. Their feats could lead to long-lasting remembrance of their gallantry. At the top of an established hierarchical honours system was the Victoria Cross, awarded to those who had displayed bravery in 'the face of the enemy'. Captain Noel Chavasse, a doctor in civilian life, was one of the war's best-known recipients. In the midst of the Battle of the Somme in 1916, Chavasse was awarded the first of two VCs. His citation, published in *The Edinburgh Gazette*, revealed how:

> He took up a party of twenty volunteers, rescued three wounded men from a shell hole twenty-five yards from the enemy's trench, buried the bodies of two officers, and collected many identity discs, although fired on by bombs and machine guns ... His courage and self-sacrifice were beyond praise.

The following year, during the Third Battle of Ypres, Chavasse was severely injured but refused to leave his post for two days. He carried the wounded to safety while under heavy fire, but was fatally injured by a shell on 2 August 1917. His citation in the *London Gazette* announced the award of his second – and posthumous – Victoria Cross. It provided a permanent, high-profile tribute to Chavasse's war service:

> By his extraordinary energy and inspiring example, he was instrumental in rescuing many wounded who would have otherwise undoubtedly succumbed under the bad weather conditions. This devoted and gallant officer subsequently died of his wounds.

Most people who died during the war did not achieve the fame or notoriety of the war's best-known heroes and martyrs. They were

A photograph of Captain Noel Chavasse, a military doctor in the Royal Army Medical Corps, attached to the King's (Liverpool) Regiment. Chavasse was awarded two Victoria Crosses for gallantry in the presence of the enemy. His second medal was awarded posthumously following his death from wounds in 1917.

remembered in hearts and minds back home, and in earnest tributes ranging from the inimitable to the much-copied. Families were also gifted a standardised, mass-produced tribute from officialdom. The British government established a committee midway through the First World War to consider the creation of a commemorative item that could be distributed to bereaved families. A small bronze plaque and accompanying scroll were settled upon as the most appropriate means to remember each life lost and to acknowledge their sacrifice 'for King and Country'.

The design of the plaque was chosen in a fiercely contested competition for British-born citizens. Civilian Edward Carter Preston's winning design was full of symbolic imagery. The icon Britannia holds a laurel wreath, a symbol of victory and honour, while a lion bites into the German Imperial eagle. The phrase 'He died for freedom and honour' was a requirement of every design submitted, with the word 'He' amended to 'She' where female volunteers were commemorated. The bronze plaque was personalised with the individual's name. Both plaque and scroll were issued alongside a printed note from the king, paying tribute to 'a brave life given for others'.

Intensive administrative efforts aimed to identify an eligible relative to receive the memorial. Despite struggles to trace addresses for eligible next of kin in 1919 and 1920, house moves, remarriage or a lack of surviving relatives complicated searches. The final tally of plaques issued was limited by a cut-off date. For deaths which occurred until 1921 families could lay claim to a plaque and scroll. However, veterans continued to die from their war wounds years later. Beyond 1921, their next of kin were ineligible.

The plaques took pride of place on the mantelpieces of hundreds of thousands of homes. Family embellishments included frames and bespoke mounts for a more personal touch. Less commonly, plaques were incorporated onto the walls of churches or embedded into community memorials. So great were the numbers issued, reflecting the severity of the war's death toll, that the plaques became commonly referred to as the 'Death Plaque', 'Dead Man's Penny' or 'Widow's Penny'. There is no known accurate figure for the total number issued.

A Next of Kin Memorial Plaque commemorating Private Ernest Tyler, who died aged 19 in September 1918. His parents had the bronze plaque and a photograph of Tyler set into this mantelpiece mount to commemorate Ernest in their London home.

THE SEARCH FOR SOLACE

A raft of enterprising companies flourished in the 1920s, offering bereaved families, veterans of the war or simply the plain curious the chance to tour the sites of bloodshed – usually at a price, although trips for the bereaved were sometimes funded by charities. Walking in soldiers' footsteps at significant locations or making pilgrimages to an Imperial War Graves Commission cemetery proved a catharsis for many relatives and veterans, offering an active way of remembering. Veteran Clifford Lane made a rather perilous visit back to the Western Front in 1920:

> I took my wife soon after we were married to Belgium and we stayed for about a week. And we wanted to find the grave of her brother, which we

did. But, in doing so, we found that it was still dangerous, very dangerous, to travel across fields and things like that because there were still shells, bombs, anything lying about. Every now and then there'd be an explosion where, I suppose, the Belgian Army were destroying live shells, you see. Every now and again people would shout to us, 'Stop! Don't come any further.' So I thought, 'To hell with this, I'm not going to risk my wife's life and my own life again!' So we stopped exploring after that.

The financial and logistical inability of so many bereaved families and friends to visit war graves was a profoundly upsetting consequence of Britain's decision not to repatriate bodies. This was especially true for the families of Empire soldiers, many of whom had journeyed to Europe across vast tracts of ocean, thousands of miles from home, to fight for the British Empire. The possibility of their families being able to visit the graves of their loved ones in Europe was severely limited.

There was another troubling aspect to grief and remembrance on a personal level. Not everybody had a family to remember them. Some soldiers had grown up without parents, raised in orphanages, and might be unmarried and childless themselves; they were not rooted in family life in the way that others had been, and so did not enjoy the same loving memorialisation. Nor did these 'outsiders' who survived benefit from family support in readjusting to life after the war and coping with what they had endured in their military service.

The families of servicemen 'shot at dawn' for desertion or for other offences, from murder to rape, also faced a challenging time. It was difficult for them to mourn their loss openly during and after the war. This often remained the case for later generations too. Due diligence was applied with regards to their burial, however, as recalled by Reginald Bryan who worked with various graves registration units:

One afternoon I had rather a sad duty to perform and that was to take a cross to put on the grave of a British soldier who had been 'shot at dawn' for supposed cowardice. He had been taken to an out of the way field surrounded by trees, with a brook running through the field, and had evidently been buried where he fell. It doesn't require very much imagination to picture the incident and I thought it all very sad that a young English soldier should have his career cut short in that way. I suppose such things are necessary in wartime, but they are very unpleasant. No one who has ever experienced the awful effects of a German bombardment or 'strafe' can fully realise what the feelings of our Tommies were — most of them having been soldiers for only a few months — and many soldiers were shot for momentarily lapses under fire as examples and deterrents to others.

The families of 306 British servicemen executed for desertion or cowardice received an official pardon in 2006. The pardon was in part explained by the then Defence Secretary Des Browne, who was 'conscious of how the families of these men feel today. They have had to endure a stigma for decades'. Men found guilty and shot for other offences, from espionage to rape or murder, were not included in the pardon.

THE SPIRITUALIST MOVEMENT

Visiting graves and former battlefields allowed an experience of 'laying to rest' the most acute grief. But there were many people who found it impossible to accept that someone had gone, or who, despite being reconciled to an individual's death, still sought to make contact with the individual in an imagined afterlife. A thriving spiritualist movement offered the bereaved an apparent means of communicating with someone they had lost.

Eminent physicist Sir Oliver Lodge was the figurehead of wartime spiritualism. His son Raymond had been killed in action in 1915, but Sir Oliver was adamant that his child had, less than a fortnight later, made contact with him via a clairvoyant. Among Sir Oliver's many publications was his wartime text *Raymond, or Life and Death* – a work roundly criticised in the press as a 'Spook Book'. But Sir Oliver was motivated by his belief that:

> The amount of premature and unnatural bereavement at the present time is so appalling that the pain caused by exposing one's own sorrow and its alleviation, to possible scoffers becomes almost negligible in view of the service which it is legitimate to hope may thus be rendered to mourners, if they can derive comfort by learning that communication across the gulf is possible.

The family of a First World War airman, Lieutenant Lewis Oertling, took great inspiration from Sir Oliver's book. They had been left confused by a muddled account about his alleged fate. Reports ranged from Oertling sustaining a broken leg in an 'accident' to going missing to being killed. Drawing blanks as they tried to investigate further, the family rallied to the idea of using a spiritual medium to help to clear up the mystery.

In a note entitled 'Information for New Sitters', Sir Oliver passed on details of a clairvoyant, Miss Ortner. He explained her methods, her price, what to expect at the 'sitting' and what those attending should bring:

A photograph of Lieutenant Lewis Oertling. His family turned to spiritualist séances in an attempt to acquire further details concerning the airman's death in service on 8 August 1918.

She generally likes some object to hold, if possible belonging to the person with whom communication is desired, if not, something belonging to the sitter.

It is best to go to the sitting with the idea in mind that this is the opportunity for those on the other side to speak. Miss Ortner now and then asks, after a description or a remark, whether the sitter can 'place it'. This does not mean that she wants information on the point, but merely that she wants to know whether the sitter is able to follow the messages or descriptions; and it is quite possible to indicate that without giving away any normal information. Miss Ortner is keen about evidence, and normal information given by the sitter merely hampers her powers.

... Do not interrupt pauses in the sitting by asking questions. During such pauses the medium is listening to messages from those on the other side; and one may break the communication by interrupting...

On visits to several different clairvoyants from 1918 into the early 1920s, the family made their own notes to compare against the comments made by each medium. When presented with Oertling's estimated age of 19 to 23, their written remarks seemed supportive: 'Age 27: but looked much younger'. When advised that Lieutenant Oertling had endured 'three weary months', the family were quick to agree: 'Yes! Very weary'. The medium relayed an impression of his last moments:

I have a feeling of falling through the air. Terrible wrench – the parting. He says – I am falling. Terrific crash on my head. Unconscious when I reached the ground. The shock that I cannot save myself causes me to lose consciousness.

Whether visits to a clairvoyant provided any genuine sense of clarity and solace is impossible to prove. Spiritualism certainly had prominent advocates. Chief among them was the novelist and writer Sir Arthur Conan Doyle. In his history of the movement, he elaborated:

The deaths occurring in almost every family in the land brought a sudden and concentrated interest in the life after death. People not only asked the question, 'If a man die shall he live again?', but they eagerly sought to know if communication was possible with the dear ones they had lost.

It is unquestionable that there were people prepared to manipulate the grief of families to their own ends. Numerous prosecutions of fraudulent mediums took place during and after the war, with fines imposed by magistrates' courts for 'fortune telling'.

LIVING WITH LOSS

Many families were unable to forget the impact of the war because of painful prosaic consequences. The financial difficulties faced by widows and their children were the cause of immense strain. While some soldiers had joined up precisely to acquire a steady wage for their families, others worried endlessly about financial hardship at home – a situation that became much worse if the breadwinner was killed. Lance Corporal Nelson Newman, who died in 1914, had shared his concerns about money with his wife back in north London:

> Well Ede don't forget that if there is anything going from the different distress funds that they are getting up put your name down as you are as much entitled to some as any one else as that is what they are getting them up for.

As well as numerous charitable funds for families suffering financial hardship, there were government pensions for widows. These consisted of an 'Alternative Pension', to be claimed if a husband's earnings before the war exceeded 25 shillings a week for the rank of private, or a flat-rate pension for the widows of men who had earned less. Applying for this financial assistance could become a very stressful matter, involving rounds of rejection and appeal.

The widow of Rifleman Bernard Bowell clashed with the Ministry of Pensions repeatedly following his death from a brain tumour in 1924. She was convinced that the cancer had developed as a result of a serious injury he had sustained during the war. In a letter to his doctor a month after his death, Mrs Bowell implored:

> My husband died on Sept 26th and I am now endeavouring to support my little girl & myself. I have applied to the Pensions Ministry for consideration on account of my husband's military service. My application would be naturally assisted if you could & would grant me a letter stating that the C T [cerebral tumour] which caused my husband's death was possibly caused or aggravated by a blow or fall.

> My husband was very severely wounded in 1917 by a bullet which passed thro' his neck causing him to fall unconscious & the point in question is whether this blow caused the growth or aggravated a growth which had hitherto lain dormant.

The channels of officialdom did not agree with Mrs Bowell's theory:

> I have to inform you that it has been decided that your husband, the late No. R/33639 Rifleman Bernard Ansell Bowell, King's Royal Rifle Corps, was not removed from duty on account of the disease of which he died, and moreover, died of a disability of which a continuous medical history has not been shown from the termination of his active service in the War, and which cannot be certified as attributable to or aggravated by such service.

> In these circumstances it is regretted that your claim to a pension cannot be admitted.

Following rounds of appeal, Mrs Bowell eventually acquired pension provision in 1927.

The war was never far from the thoughts of struggling families. Jessie Nicholson's financial plight following her husband's death in the war was laid plain in a letter from the employer of her policeman-turned-soldier husband. Chief Constable Frederick Brindley in Stockport wrote to Mrs Nicholson to commiserate and to reassure:

> I can assure you every comrade in this force, from myself downwards, has felt deeply grieved — it was a great shock to us all. He was a good and reliable policeman, cheerful in his demeanour and beloved by us all; therefore words fail me to adequately express to you our true feelings towards you and your dear little son.

> At all events, let me assure you that your loss is our loss, too; therefore it will be our one and only desire to assist you as far lies in our power to somewhat take the sting out of the wound that has so terribly been inflicted upon you.

The Chief Constable was further moved one month after the end of the war to recommend Mrs Nicholson for a job in a plaintive letter to her prospective employer:

> She is a most respectable person and has done her utmost to provide for her boy and herself without seeking outside assistance. As a matter of fact, she has been offered assistance, but has preferred to work rather than accept charity.

> I know of no soldier's widow who has worked harder than she, or who has kept herself more respectable; therefore I should regard it as a personal favour if one so deserving was successful in obtaining the position she is now seeking.

The war cast a grim shadow over individuals who had lost a parent, a spouse or a child in the conflict. Every day the absence reminded them of what they had lost. Commemorations proved of little comfort for those whose emotional resilience was destroyed by grief. Private Albert Clayden, for example, joined up in 1914; having survived years of fighting, he was killed exactly one month before the Armistice. Clayden's wife Kate struggled to cope with the devastating bereavement as well as caring for their two daughters, Evelyn and Doris. She suffered a breakdown and eventually died in a hospital for the treatment of those with mental health problems in Surrey in 1974, some 66 years after the death of her husband. After their mother's death, Evelyn and her husband arranged for Kate's ashes to be interred at Private Clayden's grave in France.

For those who received official notification of a death, confirming their status as a widow, remarriage was a possibility. A death might even spark a new relationship. In the wake of Lieutenant Alan Lloyd's death on the Somme, his widow Dorothy began a correspondence with Lieutenant Charles Marshall, one of her husband's fellow officers. The relationship blossomed, and Marshall and Dorothy became engaged in the summer of 1919. They went on to marry and have a daughter together in 1922, as well as raising David, Dorothy's son with Alan Lloyd. But for children such as David Lloyd, the war took away birth fathers they had barely known. The absence of memories became the hardest thing for many children growing up. Thousands had to rely on commemorative material rather than personal recollections to remember their fathers.

Yet memories could also be a torment. Survivors of the war who returned home with permanent war wounds also embodied a bleak, deeply personal remembrance of the First World War. The conflict's devastating violence lived on through countless individual struggles with physical rehabilitation and recovery as well as disturbing recollections of their experiences. The effects of trauma on the mind became recognised by the terms 'shell shock' and 'war neurosis'. Thousands of men were treated in hospitals, but understanding of what is now known as Post-Traumatic Stress Disorder was in its infancy. Disability, be it physical or mental, left thousands in considerable discomfort and distress long after the war was over, making it impossible to forget.

However an individual was remembered, and whatever the war's legacy for their family might be, each death that occurred as a result of the war extinguished someone unique. The deaths of relatives or friends so often caused intense and lasting personal grief. Yet this anguish was not felt in isolation. It was also the concern of a wider orbit. Communities across Britain had to adjust to the war's corrosive effects and to find ways to mark their own sense of loss.

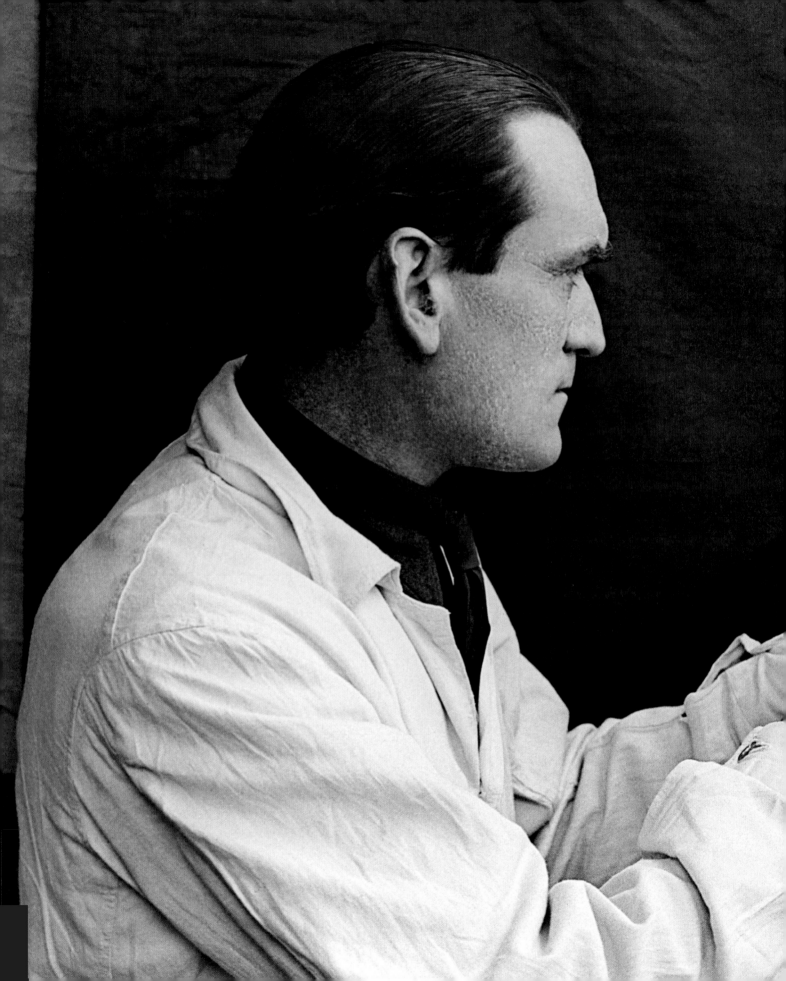

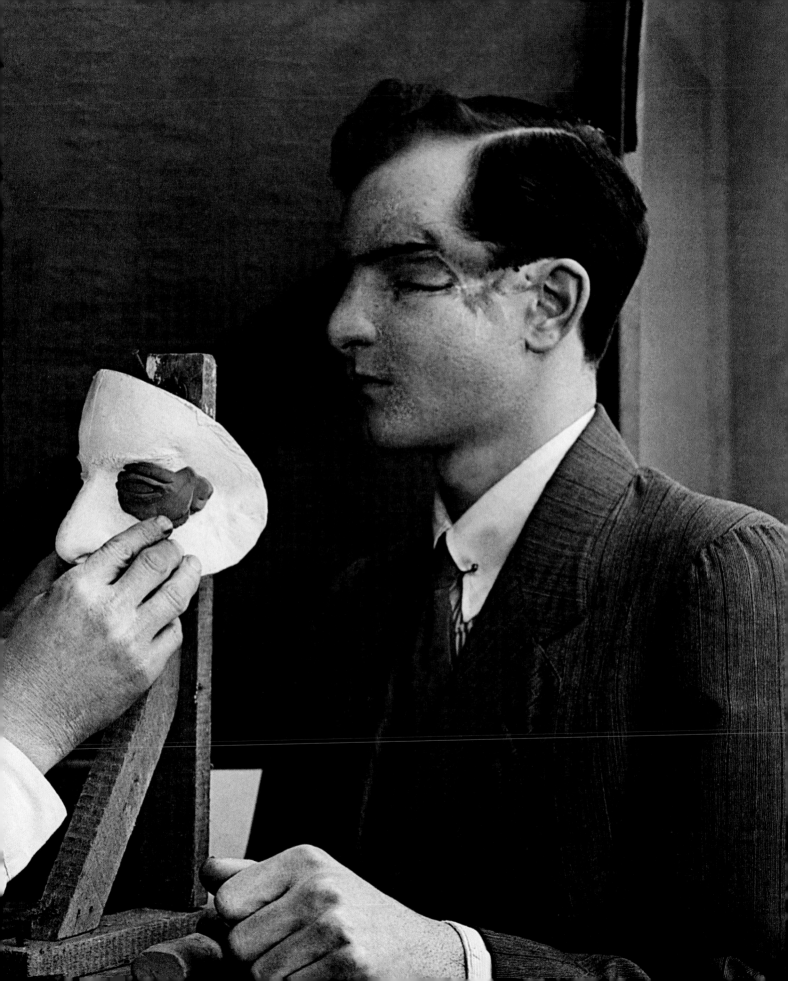

6

COMMUNITIES
REMEMBER

Although nearly nine out of ten British servicemen returned home after the First World War, the distribution of death was such that some communities were irrecoverably weakened by tragic loss. Shared identities or interests were the essence of a community, growing in places of work and worship or arising from leisure pursuits before war broke out in 1914; men had often been 'members' of more than one type of community. Mourning conventions were rocked by the authorities' decision not to bring back bodies from the fighting fronts. Yet the need to commemorate those lost in conflict was profound, and around 40,000 local war memorials were rapidly erected throughout Britain in the decade immediately after the war.

'YOUR COUNTY NEEDS YOU'

The local war memorial phenomenon was inextricably linked to the way in which the country had filled its army's ranks. Britain, with its long tradition of liberal, individual choice, was loathe to force its citizens to fight. Every other European nation at war had vast, conscripted forces for whom fighting – and potentially dying – was not a matter of choice. Yet Britain had initially to rely upon goodwill. A vigorous recruitment campaign was launched immediately upon the outbreak of war on 4 August 1914. Appeals to every conceivable motivation pushed men to leave their families, workplaces and social lives behind – for the sake of adventure, to defend their homeland, to earn a steady wage, to learn new skills and trades in the army or to inflict damage upon a hated enemy. An atmosphere of impassioned fervour at recruitment rallies resulted in some 750,000 men 'joining up' in the first eight weeks of the war.

The tentacles of recruitment tightened around local institutions as recruiting officers sought out new soldiers across the country. From football grounds and church congregations to universities, Britain became one vast enlisting ground, encompassing its highlands, islands, villages, market towns and vibrant metropolises. Men who already knew one another – whether from work, leisure activities or living in a locality – were encouraged to join so-called 'Pals Battalions'. It was hoped that an established sense of belonging would transpose smoothly into operational effectiveness, and that this unique cohesive quality might provide an asset to unit morale.

The most common bond within a new 'Pals' unit was that of a place – usually a city or a region incorporating towns, villages and isolated hamlets. But geographical identities proved complex. A place of birth did not necessarily indicate where someone had been raised. A current town of residence might mask a family's history of emigration from another place in which their real sense of identity was rooted. Battalions such as the 'Tyneside Irish' reflected a dual sense of belonging.

Opposite: A recruitment poster for one of four 'Pals' Battalions raised for the Tyneside Irish Brigade upon the outbreak of war in 1914. The Brigade was largely made up of volunteers of Irish descent who lived in Newcastle upon Tyne, reflecting the tangled identities that complicated remembrance after the war.

Previous page: Female munitions workers in Swansea walk beside the horsedrawn hearse of one of their workmates who had been killed at her work in August 1917. They wear factory uniforms in the funeral procession as a sign of belonging and respect.

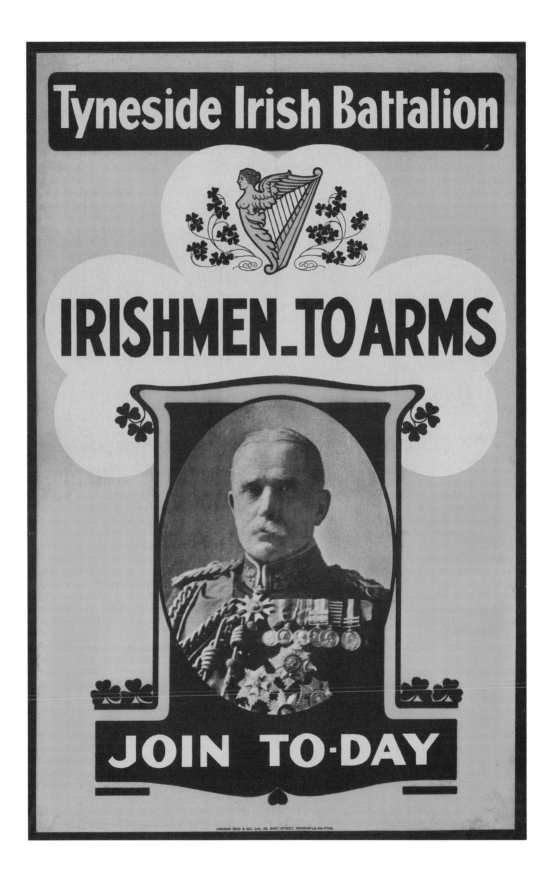

'Pals' Battalions drew upon other kinds of pre-existing camaraderie, for instance the Stockbrokers' Battalion and the Middlesex Regiment's Footballers' Battalion. More prosaically named units concealed startling unity within them. The entire first team of Edinburgh's Heart of Midlothian Football Club joined the 16th (Service) Battalion of the Royal Scots, at a time when criticism of ongoing sporting fixtures was growing, on the grounds that they were an unwelcome distraction from the war. The team's decision to join up en masse was designed, in part, to encourage similar action among Hearts fans. A club statement released in November 1914 implored supporters to follow the players' lead:

> Now then, young men, as you have followed the old club through adverse and pleasant times, through sunshine and rain, roll up in your hundreds for King and Country, for right and freedom. Don't let it be said that footballers are shirkers and cowards. As the club has become an honoured name on the football field, let it go down in history that it also won its spurs on the field of battle.

A photograph of players from the Edinburgh football club Heart of Midlothian. On 25 November 1914 the news that 11 players had joined up was announced – the first mass enlistment by a British football team. It caused a national sensation. In total 16 Hearts players volunteered, seven of whom died on active service. The club also gave the military authorities access to its ground at Tynecastle on match days to recruit volunteers from the crowd.

Seven of the Hearts players did not survive the war. They were later commemorated by a memorial in Edinburgh, the unveiling of which was attended by tens of thousands of fans.

Many thousands of women volunteered to 'do their bit' too. Having travelled to the fighting fronts, thousands of them lost their lives because of bombs dropped from planes, rogue shellings, hospital ships sinking or from illnesses such as malaria and typhus. The decision made by single women to sign up for service abroad always remained a matter of choice: all were volunteers. Married women, however, were not permitted to serve on the fighting fronts. Nursing was the foremost opportunity for female volunteers overseas. Professional career nurses were joined by Voluntary Aid Detachment (VADs) – unpaid civilian volunteers, often from relatively well-off backgrounds, who cared for the military wounded in hospitals. By 1917 men were more urgently required than ever before for fighting roles on the Western Front. Opportunities flourished in the newly formed Women's Army Auxiliary Corps for female workers in clerical work, army stores, canteens and motor transport within the range of German guns. The Women's Royal Naval Service was formed in November 1917 and the Women's Royal Air Force was set up on 1 April 1918. Over 100,000 women joined Britain's armed forces during the war.

Grim news of casualties and conditions from the fighting fronts had dampened the supply of willing male army recruits by 1915. Nevertheless, communities continued to apply coercive pressure to shame 'slackers' to join up, even though many were engaged in vital war work on the home front in coal mines, shipyards and munitions factories. By 1916 the need for manpower abroad had become so pressing that a sweeping government decision was taken to introduce compulsory military service, or conscription, for British men.

Across the Empire, the voluntary nature of recruitment was fiercely debated. Australia refused to impose conscription, while it was introduced but never imposed in Ireland. An important provision was made in Britain for those who objected on moral grounds to a front line combat role. Known as 'conscientious objectors', they were instead given roles such as stretcher bearers; often these were dangerous posts and many were killed. Only those known as 'absolutists' avoided the war fronts, with their refusal to serve in any way resulting in a prison sentence.

The years after the war saw fierce debate about the commemoration of soldiers who had served in non-combatant roles on the grounds of conscience and been killed, as well as those 'shot at dawn' for the military crime of desertion. Emotions ran high. In 1994 a Conscientious Objectors' Commemorative Stone was unveiled in London's Tavistock Square. Its inscribed dedication was 'TO ALL THOSE WHO HAVE ESTABLISHED AND ARE MAINTAINING THE RIGHT TO REFUSE TO KILL'. In 2001,

a memorial was unveiled at the National Memorial Arboretum in Staffordshire in memory of the 306 British and Empire soldiers found guilty by court martial and executed for the military crimes of desertion and cowardice. The memorial of a blindfolded young soldier awaiting his death by firing squad was inspired by Private Herbert Burden, a London teenager who had lied about his age to join up at the age of 16. He served with 1st Battalion Northumberland Fusiliers and was executed, aged 17, in 1915. Five years after the memorial's unveiling a posthumous government pardon was granted to all 306 men, reflecting increasingly inclusive attitudes towards those who had attempted to escape the fighting or been unable to function and carry out their orders.

However they came to be in the line of fire, communities said goodbye to their own for the duration of the 'emergency'. Few could imagine what that would really mean. Before that became clear, training camps across Britain forged camaraderie and regimental identity. Fledgling soldiers were cultivated into military communities before they had even made the journey over the sea to fight. They were bound by a pressing imperative to work together, fight effectively and look out for one another.

A memorial to the 306 British and Empire soldiers executed – and posthumously pardoned – for desertion and alleged cowardice at the National Memorial Arboretum in Staffordshire. Unveiled in 2001, the memorial's creation is evidence of changed attitudes towards these men, for whom the punishment had been death, nearly a century after the war.

1914 ✝ 1919

TO THE GLORIOUS MEMORY OF
THE MEN OF THIS CHURCH AND SCHOOL
WHO FELL IN THE GREAT WAR.

ZENAS E. BARNES   EDWARD POWELL
WILLIAM DINGLEY   HORACE RICHARD SMITH
GEOFFREY GOODHIND   JAMES E. TIFFIN
LEONARD GRIFFIN   WILLIAM M. WARDELL
FRANCIS S. HAMPTON   R. CYRIL WARDELL
WILLIAM McLEAN   FRED. WOOTTON

A metal memorial plaque commemorating former members of the Young Men's Bible Class of Lady Margaret Road Methodist Church, Kentish Town, London who were killed during the First World War.

COMMUNITY MEMORIALS

When the war was over, the communities these men had left were confronted by the shock of absence when they did not return. The rapidity of war memorial construction reflected the unprecedented scale of violent death; diverse tributes to the deceased were built across Britain. This was even more remarkable given that a deadly influenza epidemic killed 228,000 Britons between 1918 and 1920. Despite the gravity of this public health disaster, the flu catastrophe did not provoke the same kind of shock as did the losses sustained during the war.

Although we may take them for granted now, local memorials for the war dead were not obligatory. There was nothing forced or inevitable about the grassroots network of community action responsible for their creation. Passionate advocates strove hard to raise funds. Substantial donations from wealthy benefactors combined with heartfelt contributions from ordinary people struggling to spare any money. Committees were established to direct and drive these campaigns. Direct experience of bereavement was not a pre-requisite for involvement, although many contributors had suffered

personal loss. Lively exchanges of conflicting views often centred on how much time, money and emotional energy should be spent on remembering the dead; there were ardent promoters of memorials that would be of civic benefit for the living, especially those wounded during the war. But whenever a municipal stone memorial came to fruition, its unveiling was a major event, with the war dead celebrated as local heroes.

Community war memorials consisted of parks, gardens, village halls, plantings of trees, playing fields, memorial halls, carillons of bells, public rolls of honour and even blocks of flats dedicated to the local dead. Stockport War Memorial Art Gallery, which opened in 1925, was erected 'In memory of the people of Stockport who fell in the Great War (1914–1918)'. Today the gallery still stands or as a civic and cultural landmark to honour the 2,200 local dead whose names still adorn the walls.

Memorials for individual streets were one of the starkest reminders of how losses could devastate tight-knit neighbourhoods. Chapel Street in

Opposite, left: A programme for the opening of the Loughborough Carillon, an imposing local war memorial with 47 bells. Despite competing suggestions, a carillon tower was the preferred option to commemorate Loughborough's war dead, and the final design was funded by public donations. At the unveiling in 1923, a piece of music entitled 'Memorial Chimes' was played on the bells, having been composed for the occasion by Sir Edward Elgar.

Opposite: A poster advertising a public meeting to discuss proposals for a war memorial in Chiswick, West London. The authorities sought to create a 'dual' tribute to both the dead and the living, providing a 'lasting memorial to those who have fallen' and a source 'of permanent benefit to those who remain'.

Right: A modern memorial plaque in Chapel Street, Altrincham. It commemorates the men who volunteered as soldiers in the First World War; the original houses where they lived have now been razed.

TRAFFORD COUNCIL

CHAPEL STREET ALTRINCHAM

From just 60 houses, 161 men volunteered in the Great War 1914–1918 29 were killed.

Recognised and praised by King George V

Altrincham was called the 'bravest little street in England' by George V. During the war 60 households released 161 men to serve in the armed forces, of whom 29 died. They were commemorated in a wartime street shrine. Years after original houses had been demolished, a new plaque was unveiled in 2009 to remember the contribution of Chapel Street's First World War servicemen. Wartime memorial plaques still adorn houses in St Albans in tribute to the 110 men who lived in a small cluster of streets there and died in the First World War.

Community war memorials were not always located in populous places. The peak of England's highest mountain, Scafell Pike in the Lake District, was presented to the National Trust on behalf of the nation as a war memorial in 1919 by its owner, war veteran Lord Leconfield. A slate memorial plaque at the summit made clear that was now a place given over 'IN PERPETUAL MEMORY OF THE MEN OF THE LAKE DISTRICT WHO FELL FOR GOD AND KING, FOR FREEDOM PEACE AND RIGHT IN THE GREAT WAR'.

GEORGE WRAGGE L^{TD}

Wardry Works
152 - 156 Chapel St. Salford
MANCHESTER

LONDON
Clock House
ARUNDEL ST.
W.C. = Phone
N^o1233 Central

TELEGRAMS
"Casements"
MANCHESTER
TELEPHONE
N^o2206 Central

JMB/IW.

23th. May 1917.

Mrs. W. M. Anderson,
   62, Dover Street,
      Crumpsall,
         Manchester.

Dear Mrs. Anderson,

      On behalf of the staff of George Wragge Limited,
I wish to convey our united love and deep sympathy with you
in the loss of your dear husband, the greatest bereavement
and sorrow that can overtake womankind. Everyone here has
been deeply touched and indeed it is with great difficulty
that we can realize that it can be true.

      At such a time there is nothing that one can do
to relieve your pain, and rightly so, for yours is the greatest
loss, and your sorrow can only be measured and be equal to the
loss you have sustained. Some people think, and say, that
time is the great healer, but if you will pardon me saying so,
I think there is nothing in this world but love can make up
for our great loss, and thank God our memories are our own,
and remembrance is sweet to us all.

      We pray that God may be near to yourself and your

-1-

dear little girl, and that the light of His countenance may
rest on you, and give you that peace and understanding which
will sustain and comfort you during the rest of your life.

     Yours very sincerely,

      James M. Bolton

Workplaces were often hit hard by the loss of former employees on the fighting fronts. These pages from a condolence letter of 1917 were written to the widow of William Anderson from staff at his former employer, George Wragge Ltd in Manchester.

Although the war itself had caused many to question their faith, memorials to Christians who had been part of a congregation were a common sight in British churches. Plaques and stained-glass windows provided ornate and colourful tributes. Churches on the former fighting fronts took it upon themselves to honour British units which had been embroiled in local fighting. The Belgian village of Passchendaele was destroyed by repeated shelling; its church was rebuilt after the war and included a stained-glass memorial to the British 66th Division. The windows referenced St George, England's patron saint, and some of the English towns where the Division's soldiers came from, such as Bury, Accrington, Bolton, Blackburn and Wigan.

Employment was an enormous part of most men's lives before they 'joined up', with staff spending more time with their colleagues than their own families. Workplaces were plundered by the war's insatiable demand for manpower abroad; the employees of railways, farms, the police, banks and factories went to 'do their bit'. When employers learned a former colleague had been killed, reactions were heartfelt. Lance Corporal William Anderson, for example, was killed in the spring of 1917. In a letter to Anderson's wife on behalf of the staff at a Manchester chemical works, his colleagues expressed:

> ...our united love and deep sympathy with you in the loss of your dear husband, the greatest bereavement and sorrow that can ever overtake womankind. Everyone here has been deeply touched and indeed it is with great difficulty that we can realise that it can be true.

Bosses, supervisors and workmates across the land commiserated with families and commemorated their lost colleague's sacrifice, often in the form of a workplace memorial plaque.

It was rare that the war provided good news, but over 50 'Thankful' villages in England and Wales welcomed back safely every inhabitant who had fought. There were no such villages identified in Scotland. Memorials were erected in modest observance of the lucky feat. With so many communities grieving, however, the 'Thankful' villages were a reminder of the haphazard geographical impact of the war's slaughter.

RECUPERATING ACROSS THE SEA

Britain became a temporary home to thousands of wounded Empire troops during the conflict. Suffering serious injuries, they were transported back to Britain for treatment. These hospital communities were honoured after the war, with Brighton's Royal Pavilion the most famous example. A former Regency palace, the building was rapidly converted into a

sophisticated hospital, with X-ray machines and operating theatres. Wards accommodated up to 700 beds and some were festooned with elaborate, lotus-shaped chandeliers, reflecting the building's opulent past. Between 1914 and 1916 the hospital was used exclusively for the care of Indian soldiers. The Indian Army played a vital role in the war's early stages on the Western Front; by the end of 1914 Indian soldiers made up one-third of the British Expeditionary Force's strength.

Around 4,300 wounded Indians were transported across the English Channel and treated at the Royal Pavilion; most had never been to Britain before. The Indian Gate memorial built at the Royal Pavilion reflected the bond between the hospital community and the inhabitants of their host town. The gate was presented to the people of Brighton by the 'princes and people of India' as a gesture of thanks. At the opening ceremony on 26 October 1921 the Maharajah of Patiala praised 'Brighton's abounding hospitality', and the town's reputation as a place of healing was celebrated across India. The Chattri memorial in nearby countryside marked the site where Hindus and Sikhs from the hospital who had succumbed to wounds or illness were cremated. The Muslim dead were buried in a cemetery in Woking, the designated place of burial for soldiers of the faith who had died at the Royal Pavilion and elsewhere along the south coast, near to what was then Britain's only dedicated mosque.

CONTINUING COMRADESHIP

After the war, surviving soldiers from Britain and across the Empire headed home. There they confronted the difficult task of reintegrating with their families and friends, and finding new employment in a changed world. Friction within communities grew. Former volunteers and conscripts had been through experiences unimaginable to many back home, even the well-meaning and empathetic. A homecoming, anticipated for so long, could be an anti-climax in reality. Returning veteran Raynor Taylor's brother, Albert, had trouble acclimatising to life with his family after demobilising:

> Our Albert, in particular, he used to go up in the town... because after demobilisation in 1919, it says a lot for the British character that there wasn't a mutiny or something. Because there were so many soldiers coming back into civilian life who'd been tied down by strict discipline for years, so there was a tendency for them to be ... they went pretty

mad at times. Our Albert, he got friendly with some and yes, he never came home drunk or anything like that but they [his parents] didn't like the type of people that he was associating with. But they were people he'd been in the army with; he'd done four years with them. And I remember one night he must have been in bother or something and he came home and he'd got the loveliest black eye you've ever seen in your life ... it was a beauty! My dad looked at him, my mother began to cry. My dad looked at him, he said, 'Serves thee right', he said, and that was all!

Veterans' associations were established in response to the need to create a supportive, understanding community of former servicemen. Staying in touch became a form of 'living' remembrance. The Old Contemptibles Association, formed in 1925, was the most famous British group of this kind, its name deriving from an Order of the Day issued by the German Kaiser in 1914 which had referred derisively to Britain's 'contemptible little army'. All ranks of the British Expeditionary Force who served on the front line in France and Belgium between 5 August and 22 November 1914 were entitled to brand themselves an 'Old Contemptible', adopting the insult with tongue-in-cheek pride. The association eventually flourished into 178 branches at home, with a further 14 overseas. It produced its own magazine and all members were referred to as 'chums'.

Veterans' associations organised reunions for those who had fought, worked, endured, suffered and – sometimes – enjoyed the war together. As the tone of public remembrance became increasingly sombre, the raucous nature of some regimental association dinners attracted criticism. When they met up, veterans remembered their lost comrades, but they also celebrated a shared sense of community, humour and their own survival, often with lashings of alcohol.

Veterans also spearheaded an unusual form of tourism as another way of remembering their own experiences. Battlefield tours became extremely popular in the 1920s for both ex-servicemen and families of the war dead. These trips were dependent on private wealth. For those unable to afford the journey, charitable assistance was available through pilgrimages organised by the YMCA, Church Army, Salvation Army and St Barnabas Society. Accommodation was provided in the form of army huts converted into hostels for pilgrims. William Cowley was a member of the Gallipoli Association and made a memorable trip back to the peninsula with the group:

Well it's a comradeship, you know, and I meet some of the old boys when I go up there. In fact, I went to Gallipoli, you know, ten years ago. We had a party and my son went – he's an associate member of the association ....
And we toured the Dardanelles, went to Cape Helles and all around Anzac

A poster by the Young Man's Christian Association highlighting the problems faced by servicemen after the war. Many had suffered permanent wounds and struggled to reintegrate and find employment.

and eventually Suvla Bay. I saw the old beach of course, nobody living there. I could see it; see the beach where we landed. I brought some souvenirs home. I brought a bit of a fig tree and a bit of some stones off the beach. It was marvellous.

Regimental identity was so important to the British Army that a forest of memorials reflective of these deliberately distinct communities were built at home and abroad in areas where units had notably served. Tributes ranged from the magnificent, like the Royal Artillery Memorial at London's Hyde Park Corner, to the delicate and curious, such as a memorial lamp.

As the twentieth century wore on, veterans of the First World War began to age and pass away. There remained a small number of extraordinarily elderly veterans at the turn of the millennium, rendered by longevity into the mouthpieces of a fading generation. But outstanding age also began to isolate them from the community of comrades they had once been part of. Harry Patch, born in 1898, became the longest surviving former British combat soldier of the First World War. He died in 2009, aged 111 years old. In one of many interviews given in his centenarian years, Patch explained his surprise: 'Millions of men came to fight in this war and I find it incredible that I am the only one left.' There are now no surviving veterans of the First World War, and the loss of this living link has given renewed focus to the issue of how best to remember the conflict moving forward.

Above left: A badge of the Old Contemptibles Association. Such associations were important support mechanisms for ex-servicemen, enabling veterans to keep the memory of their service and comradeship alive. All ranks of the British Expeditionary Force who served on the Western Front within range of enemy fire between 5 August and 22 November 1914 were entitled to call themselves 'Old Contemptibles'.

Above: A 'Lamp of Remembrance' for deceased comrades. This unusual tribute from a veterans' association is inscribed: 'To the memory of those of the 60th (London) Divisional Cyclists' Company, who fell in the Great War 1914–1918 and to those who have died since.'

CIVILIAN CASUALTIES

Deaths attributable to the conflict were not just the preserve of those in the military or volunteer forces abroad. Bombing raids and industrial accidents in munitions factories were responsible for thousands of civilian deaths. Early in the war, people were targeted in a shocking assault on coastal towns on England's east coast. German ships blasted the towns of Scarborough, Hartlepool and Whitby on 16 December 1914. Over 100 men, women and children were killed and over 450 wounded. The attacks prompted outrage and were used as a spur to army recruitment.

Fatal German air attacks ensured that British people could no longer feel a sense of complacency and security because of the sea barrier with Europe. In the First World War German air raids caused nearly 2,000 deaths, killing men, women and children with bombs and shells on home ground. The south-east of England suffered especially from air raids, owing to its geographical proximity to German airfields, but Zeppelin airships achieved fatal strikes on civilians as far north as Edinburgh.

Unlike deaths on the fighting fronts, people killed by German air attacks on Britain were often afforded major funerals, well attended by their communities. Upper North Street School in Poplar was attacked in the first daylight aeroplane air raid on London, which occurred on 13 June 1917. A single bomb killed 18 children, most of whom were just five years old. The raid was perceived as an outrage – indelible proof of the barbarism of the Germans. A week later 15 of the child victims were buried in a mass grave in an elaborate funeral; the public sent over 600 wreaths. The children's coffins were moved by horse-drawn hearses past houses with blinds drawn down and the thousands of people who had gathered in the streets. Flags flew at half-mast and George V and Queen Mary issued a personal message to be read out at the service. The congregation was full of children who had survived the blast.

Mementos were produced to commemorate the tragedy, with funds raised towards a convalescent care fund for survivors and a permanent stone memorial. This was unveiled in 1919 at the cemetery where the mass burial had taken place. A slew of memorial cards made much of the perceived German barbarism. One read:

'SUFFER LITTLE CHILDREN TO COME UNTO ME'
'FOR SUCH IS THE KINGDOM OF HEAVEN'
Those tiny school babes, our little ones,
Had ceased their task and were listening with bated breath,
For the blotting out of the glorious sun
By the broken thunder of the German Death.

Victims were remembered through propaganda as well as through outpourings of grief. Mimic replicas of the German Iron Cross for bravery were commercially produced in Britain to commemorate, with bitter irony, the 'battle honours' of 'war atrocities'. A similar effort was made following the outrage that greeted the sinking of the passenger liner RMS *Lusitania*, the subject of some of the most haunting propaganda of the war. The ship was torpedoed by a German submarine off the south-west coast of Ireland on its return to Liverpool from New York. Nearly 1,200 people were killed, most of them civilians. It is now known that the vessel was carrying munitions as part of its cargo, a fact insisted upon by Germany during the war in justifying the attack on the liner. The dangerous haul was unconfirmed at the time in Britain and for many subsequent decades.

Industrial accidents on the home front claimed further civilian lives. Colossal new factories were built to churn out vast quantities of weapons, equipment and supplies; a vast site at Gretna, at the border between England and Scotland, included the construction of a 'township' of houses, nurseries, a cinema, bank and shops. When off-duty, people were sustained and entertained without needing to stray far. Older factories were also converted for the production of high-explosive shells. In the haste to produce munitions, converted factories in densely habited urban locations posed a great danger to their surroundings. Intended to kill and maim enemy troops abroad, their lethal output killed many workers at home instead. On 19 January 1917 a catastrophic explosion ripped through the Brunner Mond and Company's high-explosive TNT factory in Silvertown, London. Fireman J J Betts recalled the blast's devastating impact:

> It was as though heaven had giddily plunged to meet the earth in a shattering upheaval... Around me was a vast plain of rubble. The factory had gone. There were fearful sounds in the air, the screams of injured women and children, the groans of those imprisoned under the debris...

The explosion killed 73 people, including children in nearby houses, and injured hundreds more. The community was catapulted into mourning, and ultimately into memorialisation. Cards were printed to commemorate the event, one giving difficult details of the carnage inflicted:

> Pathetic Incidents.

> Heartrending scenes were witnessed at Poplar Hospital, where casualties began to arrive shortly after the disaster.

Women, and men too, were moved to tears as they watched the bodies, some limbless and some almost lifeless, lifted from the ambulances and carried by the Red Cross into the building.

Most of the poor victims were unconscious, and many had passed beyond human aid by the time the hospital gates were reached.

Right: A 'souvenir' napkin to commemorate the teachers and children killed in the air raid on Upper North Street School in 1917. Such commemorative items were often produced to mark notable losses of civilian life as a result of the war.

Below right: A cortege makes its way down a street lined by mourners in East London. The funeral procession was for 15 child victims of a German bomb, dropped on Upper North Street School in Poplar in June 1917.

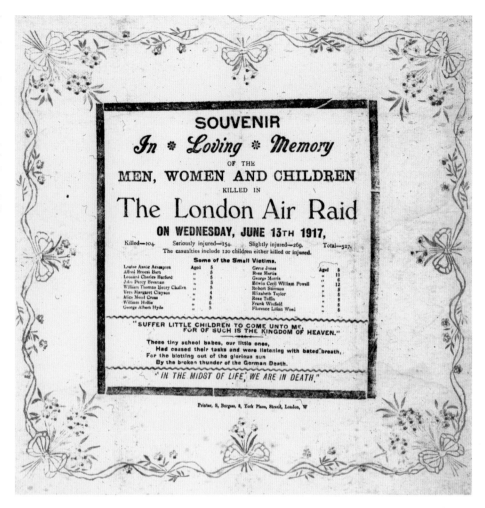

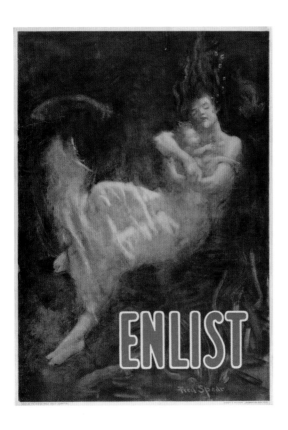

Extensive new factories were far from safe despite their recent construction. A mighty explosion at the gigantic National Shell Filling Factory at Chilwell, Nottinghamshire resulted in the deaths of 134 workers on 1 July 1918. The factory produced over half of Britain's total output of high-explosive shells during the First World War. So ferocious was the blast that only 32 bodies could be positively identified. The dead workers were commemorated by a memorial unveiled in March 1919 which also detailed the factory's achievements in supplying the forces with deadly firepower. Weeks before the deadly accident employees had set a national record, when workers filled 46,725 shells in one 24-hour period on 15 June 1918.

Whether killed in action, dying from wounds in a field station, in a hospital bed back home or in bombing assaults on their own homes, the war dead were mourned and remembered by British communities. Although many were depleted by loss, and had even become battlegrounds themselves, the war instigated a burst of creativity within communities; new forms of mourning were established and memorials for shared identities and places were eagerly designed and constructed. This spontaneous, grassroots endeavour contrasted with the formal rituals of remembrance imposed by the government to represent the grief of an entire nation.

Above left: An American recruitment poster, dramatically illustrated with a drowning woman. The sinking of the passenger liner RMS *Lusitania*, torpedoed by a German submarine in 1915 with the loss of nearly 1,200 lives, generated many commemorative pieces. It was also used as a recruiting spur in Britain and later the United States upon its entry to the war in 1917, so palpable was outrage generated by the German sinking of the passenger liner.

Above: A mock German Iron Cross, designed to deride the 'battle honours' awarded to their troops for carrying out attacks on British and European civilians. This example commemorates the bombardment of Hartlepool, Scarborough and Whitby from the sea by the German Navy on 16 December 1914. Over 100 civilians were killed in these coastal towns and some 450 were wounded. Commercially produced propaganda pieces kept the memory of the attack alive.

Stockpiles of high explosive shells in the National Shell Filling Factory at Chilwell, Nottinghamshire in August 1917. Britain's most productive factory of its kind, in 1918 Chilwell was the scene of a huge explosion in which 134 workers died. It was the biggest loss of life sustained through a single explosion on the home front during the First World War.

COMRADESHIP AND REMEMBRANCE

Among the old comrades' organisations that were formed across Britain in the aftermath of the First World War, the Salonika Reunion Association (SRA) was unique. It did not focus its membership around a particular regiment, unit or formation, nor was membership open to any former serviceman in the manner of the British Legion. Instead those joining the SRA had to have served in the Balkans with British forces between 1915 and 1919. This made the SRA the only British campaign-specific veterans' organisation until the formation of the Burma Star Association in 1951.

Although 228,000 military personnel served with the British Salonika Force (BSF) during the First World War, their contribution to victory was quickly forgotten with the signing of the Armistice on 11 November 1918. In Britain the Salonika campaign was generally viewed as a peripheral military commitment, under-resourced in terms of manpower, munitions and equipment. Despite these handicaps the BSF and other Allied contingents contended with difficult terrain, extremes of summer and winter climate, poor lines of communications and endemic malaria to defeat the battle-hardened Bulgarian Army. Yet these achievements were little reported in the newspapers and the campaign was denigrated in Britain through a music hall song containing the line 'If you don't want to fight, go to Salonika'.

With their wartime contribution overlooked and vanishing from popular memory, former members of the BSF took matters into their own hands. The first move came in early 1922 when Major Elliot Bell contacted General Sir George Milne, former commander of the BSF, and proposed an annual dinner for former officers. Those attending donated funds towards a wreath to be laid at the Cenotaph in London. Two years later the decision was taken to open up the wreath laying to all interested BSF veterans. Following a good turn-out at the commemoration, an idea was put forward that former other ranks should be able to contribute to the wreath and attend the annual dinner. Milne agreed and asked Major Bell to organise the 1925 event on these lines.

The resulting parade on Sunday 4 October 1925 saw 1,500 BSF veterans, including former nurses and VADs, attend the Cenotaph; 600 of them went on to a dinner. With so much interest from veterans it was a short step to the formation of the Salonika Reunion Association. The donation towards a wreath became an annual subscription, and by 1937 the SRA had almost 3,000 members.

The central objective of the SRA was to reunite former comrades and foster the wartime spirit forged during the Salonika campaign. A central committee administered the association and organised an annual ceremony of commemoration on either 30 September, if a Sunday, or the first Sunday in October. This key event in the SRA calendar involved a service of remembrance,

---

Opposite: Members of the Yorkshire Branch of the Salonika Reunion Association attending their annual dinner at the City Arms Hotel in York on 19 October 1946.

Membership badge of the Salonika Reunion Association. The design shows the sun rising above the mountains of northern Greece, fronted by the blue of the Aegean Sea.

The standard of the Salonika Reunion Association, present at all national SRA events and commemorations. Following the disbanding of the Association in 1969, the standard was presented to the Imperial War Museum.

wreath laying at the Cenotaph and a dinner or social gathering. Named 'Salonika Sunday', the event centred around a gathering of veterans on Horse Guards Parade. The focus of the day was comradeship and commemoration of those who did not return from the front. Reports on 'Salonika Sunday' in the pages of the December 1928 edition of the SRA's quarterly magazine, *The Mosquito*, emphasised these objectives, which lay at the heart of the Association. In an article entitled 'The Great Day', the event's emotional purpose was made clear:

> Side by side we still stand, united as in those grim, eventful days, survivors of a campaign, the difficulties, sufferings, and achievements of which we and our absent comrades alone fully appreciate. We are here not for pomp and pageantry, but to grasp hands in perpetuation of that comradeship which has deepened as the years have passed. There is a still nobler purpose – to pay homage to the memory of those who lie in a far-off country, who today live again in the hearts of their old pals.

The Annual Muster provided the main opportunity for members across the country to meet. Attendance was encouraged by the Committee and the pages of *The Mosquito* often carried advice on travel options, calls for London-based members to provide accommodation for those travelling long distances and for wealthier members to subsidise travel for their less well-off comrades. By 1933 attendance at the event stood at around 2,500 veterans. As SRA membership grew, from 1932 parades and wreath layings were held on 'Salonika Sunday' in a number of towns and cities around the country. These took place at the same time as events in London, allowing those members unable to travel to the capital to feel part of the Association's special day.

To ensure members continued to see themselves as part of a special group, the SRA spread and maintained its ethos through a network of regional branches. Local branches were the building blocks of the SRA, with members organised into them for the Annual Muster parade on 'Salonika Sunday'. Branch meetings were the forum where ex-BSF men and women could get together on a regular basis and join in a range of activities and social functions, from dinners, dances and quiz nights to day trips and children's parties. With family members encouraged to participate in many of the events, these proved to be true bonding experiences, bringing relatives rather than just individual veterans together.

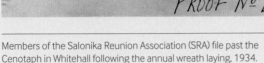

Members of the Salonika Reunion Association (SRA) file past the Cenotaph in Whitehall following the annual wreath laying, 1934.

Field Marshal Lord Milne and Brigadier Kelly inspect a group of former VADs during the Salonika Reunion Association's annual muster on Horse Guards Parade, 6 October 1929.

Branches also raised money and investigated cases for the Association's benevolent fund and helped to organise other fundraising efforts. Always looking to expand the membership, the Association's committee fostered a spirit of competition between branches. From 1929 the White Tower trophy was awarded annually to the branch that achieved the highest paid-up membership. In addition, from 1938 the various London branches competed in a similar manner for the Comradeship Cup.

Alongside branch meetings, the main source of information for SRA members was the Association's quarterly magazine, *The Mosquito*. Beginning life in September 1927 as the newsletter of the West London Branch, by issue No.4 in December 1928 the publication had gone national. As well as disseminating news of SRA activities, especially the Annual Muster in London, *The Mosquito* reported on the Association's AGM, its benevolent fund and the activities of the branches. Also posted in its pages were updates on individual members, including births, marriages, deaths and changes of address.

One regular column, 'Lost Trails', aimed to help old comrades re-establish contact. From the September 1931 edition a section called 'The Woman's Pages' was included. This ensured the growing number of female members of the SRA had a clear voice in the publication,

although they could, of course, contribute to any section of the magazine. During the Great Depression *The Mosquito* also acted as a support mechanism for Salonika veterans; it carried adverts for businesses run by former BSF men and women and encouraged members to support old comrades when possible through the harsh economic times.

Much of the language found in the pages of the magazine aimed to forge a special identity for SRA members. Typical of the phraseology used was the 'Brotherhood of the Balkans' and the 'Salonika Spirit... forged in the fields of fever, flies and filth'. Members themselves were often referred to as 'Old Salonikans', bound together by their wartime experiences: 'Those who bear the Salonika brand will be forever blood brothers and sisters.' Likewise the Annual Muster was called a 'day of immortal memories', a day when 'We, the remnants of the Salonika Army, remind the outside world of our existence'.

Many of the articles found within editions of *The Mosquito* had the effect of reinforcing a Salonika identity. These included accounts of the fighting at Doiran and in the Struma Valley, the surrender of Bulgaria in 1918, reminiscences about army food, bivouac tents, the flora and fauna of Macedonia, songs sung by the BSF and the sights, sounds and smells of Salonika.

Members of the Salonika Reunion Association drawn up on Horse Guards Parade during the annual muster, 2 October 1928.

As an organisation the SRA was given added legitimacy through the active involvement of former senior officers of the BSF. Field Marshal Lord Milne held the position of Patron from the formation of the Association until his death in 1948. This placed the veterans under their old commander, making membership of the SRA something akin to continuing their wartime service. Milne, known to members under his wartime nickname 'Uncle George', was a very hands-on Patron. From his involvement with the establishment of the Association, he attended functions whenever possible, rarely missed the Annual Muster and visited many SRA branches. In December 1942 *The Mosquito* declared that no other senior military officer could claim such an intimate friendship with those who had served under his command. When speaking at SRA events Milne stressed the value of comradeship, remembrance

and the importance of maintaining the ethos of the old British Salonika Force.

The SRA was also ambitious enough to plan pilgrimage tours to the former Salonika Front. However, organising such visits to the Balkans proved much more difficult than the equivalent cross-Channel journey to places such as Ypres and the Somme. Distance and the associated factors of time and cost told against such plans. After SRA members took part in a successful pilgrimage to Gallipoli and Salonika organised by the St Barnabas Society in 1928, the Association attempted to organise its own trip. A plan to charter the liner *City of Paris* in 1934 proved over-ambitious as too few members were able to afford the minimum fare.

Undeteterred by this failure, a new pilgrimage was proposed for 1936. Like the earlier St Barnabas trip this would be a joint Gallipoli–Salonika venture, immediately

Veterans of the British Salonika Force take part in the service of remembrance during the SRA's annual muster on Horse Guards Parade, 1934.

opening the tour up to a wider potential pool of travellers. The cruise aboard the liner *Lancastria* would last 22 days. Its promise of cheaper 'all-in' fares covering meals and excursions as well as accommodation brought the voyage within reach of many more veterans. The SRA marketed the tour in the pages of *The Mosquito* as the best-ever chance for members to visit the old battlefields in company of old comrades. It proved very successful. Excursions were offered to key sites associated with the BSF, including the Imperial War Graves Commission (IWGC) cemeteries and the Doiran Memorial, and meetings with Greek and Yugoslav veterans also took place.

Although no pilgrimage on this scale was repeated by the SRA, smaller tour groups set out for the Balkans by train and coach in the aftermath of the Second World War, once the political situation had settled

down in Europe. All such battlefield visits were reported in *The Mosquito* to keep members in touch with their wartime haunts.

As well as commemorating fallen comrades and providing a way to keep the spirit of comradeship alive, the SRA worked to assist former members of the BSF and their families in hardship. This it did through a benevolent fund established in 1928. The fund was administered by a central committee with money coming from the annual interest of a trust fund, topped up by donations gathered during the Annual Muster and at regional branch meetings. As money was relatively limited, a strict set of criteria laid down that where a case was appropriate for assistance by another established organisation the claimant should be directed to the existing body. However, those so referred were eligible for top-up awards from the SRA benevolent fund.

Copies of *The Mosquito* (1965, 1966 and 1968), a professionally produced journal at the heart of the Salonika Reunion Association. It offered members a place to record their wartime reminiscences, enabled old comrades to keep in touch and provided news of events and activities.

In addition, except under exceptional circumstances, assistance would not be given to cover financial loans, legal costs, funeral expenses, retrospective medical bills or rent arrears. Serving members of the armed forces were also not eligible, nor were their wives and dependants; nor were individuals receiving any form of poor relief. Nor was money made available as maternity grants or to cover the cost of travel to visit relatives in hospital or war graves. Yet, despite this lengthy list of restrictions, the fund made a real difference to the lives of many Salonika veterans and their families. It contributed towards the purchase of invalid carriages, hearing aids, interview suits and specialist work tools. The fund prided itself on the fact that, unlike large organisations with a heavy case load, it was able to take time over each claim and ensure attention to detail.

Although not functioning as an employment agency, the Salonika Force Benevolent Fund included a large number of requests from individuals in search of work during the late 1920s and 1930s. Committee members were happy to place such requests before other organisations dealing with employment. In

addition, especially throughout the Great Depression, the Honorary Secretary of the fund committee requested that members of the SRA inform him of any job opportunities which could be offered to needy veterans.

One particular case highlighted in the pages of *The Mosquito* during 1930 was that of Private Alfred Canning, a former member of the 7th Royal Berkshires. Canning suffered from partial paralysis in both legs brought on by severe rheumatism, which he argued was due to his military service. With a wife and two children to support, Canning was receiving Poor Law relief while the British Legion fought for two years to get him a war pension. Disagreement between doctors at his medical boards led to the Ministry of Pensions turning down his application, as it had not been proved that his condition was due to his service in Salonika. While appealing the Ministry's decision, Canning received short-term assistance from the Salonika Force Benevolent Fund. His only income at that time came from selling socks which he manufactured on a knitting machine purchased by the British Legion. As Canning lived in an isolated rural village and could not travel, the market for his socks was limited.

This carved stick, named 'Uncle George' after Field Marshal Lord Milne, was found in Macedonia during the Salonika Campaign. It was presented to Lord Milne in 1926 by former British Salonika Force officers. At Milne's request the stick was used as an emblem of office by the SRA Chairmen at AGMs and other formal occasions.

Salonika veterans outside St Peter's Church in Eaton Square, London on 26 June 1960 before the SRA's annual service of remembrance. The final meeting of the SRA took place in 1968.

The SRA told Canning's story in *The Mosquito* and encouraged members to purchase his socks. Adverts for Canning's creations appeared in editions of *The Mosquito* until 1939. In such ways the BSF family looked after its own.

Much of the success of the SRA was due to a core group of individuals who devoted much time and energy to the Association. Brigadier General H Kelly was initial Vice President and later President of the SRA; he was also the first Chair of the benevolent fund. Kelly, along with Major Elliot Bell, played a central role in establishing the SRA and personally took up many of the cases coming before the benevolent fund. Mr G E Willis served as editor of *The Mosquito* from June 1933, and it was thanks to his efforts that the SRA's magazine continued to appear as a quality quarterly journal during the Second World War. Willis went on to serve as one of the last Vice Presidents of SRA. Miss Aileen Moore served as long-time editor of 'The Woman's Pages' in *The Mosquito*. She coordinated many activities for ex-nursing sisters and VADs, ensuring that female members of the SRA maintained a strong presence in the organisation.

Up to the outbreak of the Second World War the branch network expanded rapidly. Then many Salonika veterans re-joined the armed forces or took up other war work, resulting in the disbanding of branches in Liverpool, Malaya and Malta. The Muster in London, an event at the centre of the SRA calendar, did not take place between 1938 and 1945 owing to the Munich Crisis and Second World War. There was a fear that the entire SRA would fold, but it endured. Captain F W Wilson-Hill, who served as Honorary Liaison Secretary from 1937, became the main point of contact between the SRA Committee and local branches, promoting and encouraging membership; 13 new branches formed during the Second World War. Wilson-Hill's activities in communicating with members and visiting branches proved critical to the SRA's survival. In the midst of a new global conflict, its veterans apparently wished to preserve their original sense of comradeship as a source of strength. By 1947, when the Malta Branch reformed, there were 62 regional and 16 affiliated branches forming the SRA. The commemorative London Muster resumed after the war and continued until the disbanding of the Association.

The *Mosquito* continued to publish during the Second World War, keeping members up to date with news of the fighting in, and subsequent occupation of, those nations in which they had served. The continuing feeling of affinity with the Balkans led the SRA to undertake fund-raising activities during and after the Second World War. Despite the chaos of civil war in Greece after 1945, the SRA was determined to do something constructive in Thessaloniki to forge a lasting link between the Association and the city to which the SRA owed its existence. Through the Greek Red Cross Town and Village Adoption Scheme the Association agreed to sponsor a school in the city, raising money to help rebuild crumbling classrooms. The Association, via its branches, also collected and purchased school equipment, textbooks, sports kit, general stationery and clothing for pupils, all of which were in desperately short supply in Greece.

In 1951 the SRA went further and 'adopted' the village of Mavropalgia in northern Greece. Formerly known as Karamudli, the village had served as a brigade headquarters for the BSF and was therefore well known to many veterans. Through monetary donations the Association was responsible for financing the first piped water supply to reach the village and the replacement of the church roof. Other funds provided the villagers with clothing, first aid equipment, school stationery, kitchen utensils, sewing machines and hand tools. Both these adoption schemes remained at the heart of the SRA until it finally disbanded in 1969.

The decision taken to wind up the Association in March 1969 was made with a heavy heart and after more than two hours of deliberation at the 1966 AGM. By the late 1960s age was wearying the veterans, and it was proving harder to replace key individuals at national committee and local branch level. Although

A selection of Salonika Reunion Association Christmas cards. All place a significant emphasis on remembrance as well as Christmas greetings.

new members were still joining, giving the Association a membership of around 2,000 in 1966, almost all were aged over 70 years of age. At the final annual muster on Horse Guards Parade on 6 October 1968, the fiftieth anniversary of the end of the First World War, 1,200 members answered the call to commemorate their fallen comrades one final time. However, despite the disbanding of the SRA, a number of more active veterans formed the Salonika Society and met twice a year in London until 1990. Then, after 68 years of remembrance and commemoration from the first act in 1922, the veterans of the British Salonika Force marched no more.

Throughout its 44-year existence the SRA provided British Salonika Force veterans with a forum in which to remember their wartime experiences, maintain friendships and commemorate comrades who died in the Balkans. The Association remained a non-political and non-militant organisation. By setting up its own

benevolent fund the Association was, in a way, echoing the self-reliance of the BSF, always under-resourced by the War Office. Throughout its existence the SRA worked successfully in formal and informal ways to foster a lasting spirit of comradeship and remembrance of the Salonika war dead among its membership.

ALAN WAKEFIELD
Head of First World War
IWM

7

NATIONAL
REMEMBRANCE

The First World War was fought in defence of 'King and Country'. The subsequent human cost was marked by a variety of commemorative ceremonies and monuments established by the governments of Britain and its Empire. As years went by, rituals of remembrance formalised by the state became enduring cornerstones of public life. While private and community expressions of grief and remembrance developed organically and were often diverse, state memorialisation had to reflect the feelings of millions, from the personally bereaved to the interested onlooker. It also had to ensure relevance and resonance with future generations who had not known the war.

Nearly one million servicemen from Britain and its Empire, along with thousands of female volunteers, died during the war. As with every sphere of remembrance, from private homes to centres of political power, the unprecedented scale of death and the decision not to repatriate bodies crucially influenced the way in which the war dead were commemorated. A quagmire of conflicting opinions dogged government decisions about how the war's death toll should be commemorated.

THE END OF THE WAR

The solemn forms of state remembrance that evolved were in many ways at odds with how the war's end was received at the time. Rapture, relief and disbelief greeted the day the fighting ended: 11 November 1918. This conclusion followed dramatic swings in fortune between the Allies and the Central Powers. Following a last gasp offensive that began in March and lasted until July, the German Army was finally and decisively beaten on the battlefield by November. Any support from its allies had collapsed. With the home front crumbling, beset by chronic food shortages and political turmoil and facing a resurgent Allied effort on the battlefield, the German High Command reluctantly requested the terms of an end to the fighting – an Armistice. Yet troops on the front line were relatively isolated from up-to-date news of the war's wider context. William Davies of the Machine Gun Corps had trouble convincing his battalion of his discovery during a spell of leave:

> In Paris, I could see the continental *Daily Mail* and from it I gathered that the war was virtually over. I got back to the unit and said, 'This war's nearly over' and they would not believe me. They said it was absolutely ridiculous – not in that language – because there were lorries pouring, troops, ammunition incessantly. It was all going on as if we had to go all the way to Cologne, you see...

But no one was going to Cologne. The terms of the Armistice were signed on behalf of the German delegation by Secretary of State Matthias Erzberger at 5am on 11 November 1918 in the railway carriage of the Commander of the Allied forces, Marshal Ferdinand Foch, in the remote French forest of Compiègne. The grudging acquiescence that Germany could no longer fight on came into force six hours later at 11am. The conditions the ceasefire imposed made it impossible for the German Army to recommence fighting. German soldiers had to evacuate invaded territories and surrender weapons, including 5,000 artillery pieces and 25,000 machine guns. Kaiser Wilhelm II had abdicated and a democratic government was formed in Germany. At last the bloodshed was over.

Yet only six months later, with the signing of the Treaty of Versailles, was the peace formalised. In Britain the date the fighting stopped, rather than the later date when the war formally ended, became the calendar fixture of remembrance. The Armistice anniversary went on to become enshrined in British public life.

Before the peace negotiations had even reached a close, Allied success was celebrated. Troops from the far reaches of the Empire, who had been transferred to Britain from the former fighting fronts but were yet to return to their own homes, marched through London in triumph on 3 May 1919. A committee was set up in the same month to consider how Britain would mark the moment when the war formally came to a close and peace was delivered. Ideas ranged along a celebratory spectrum. After considering a four-day extravaganza, with simultaneous celebrations in London and Paris, it was decided to restrict British events to a single occasion. When the Treaty of Versailles was signed on 28 June 1919, 'Peace Day' was rapidly planned to follow on its heels. An official statement declared that 19 July had been chosen for a 'general celebration of the Conclusion of Peace'. It would also include recognition of the colossal loss of life the British war effort had entailed.

Celebrations were organised across the country and Empire. The focal point was London, capital of the British Empire. Nearly 15,000 Allied and imperial troops took part in a victory parade as crowds thronged the streets. The British, French and American Allied commanders Haig, Foch and Pershing led the parade. The British Prime Minister David Lloyd George was insistent that there should be a tribute to the dead. In early July the celebrated architect Sir Edwin Lutyens had been hastily commissioned to design a monument where the war dead could be saluted as part of the day's events. Lutyens' suggestion of a Cenotaph, or 'empty tomb', where this could take place at the parade's final point, was agreed. That same day, over dinner, the architect hastily drafted sketches of his idea.

Within a fortnight, a towering wood and plaster construction based on Lutyens' concept was built in readiness for the 'Peace Day' spectacle. The monument became an immediate focus for national anguish over the scale of lives lost and the inability to bury most of the dead back home. At that point, however, the structure was intended to stand only for one week. No one had imagined how dramatically the wooden Cenotaph would capture the popular imagination. Floral bouquets accumulated into a mountainous pile as crowds jostled to place their own tributes. *The Times* described the design as 'so grave, severe and beautiful that one might wish it were indeed of stone and permanent'. Foreign Minister Lord Curzon, who had strongly advocated the celebratory feel of the 'Peace Day', described the Cenotaph as 'an imperial monument commemorating men of all races and creeds'. So overwhelming was the demand to visit the structure that the temporary Cenotaph was left in situ to weather the elements until January 1920, when it was finally removed. The wooden top was retained and displayed at the recently founded Imperial War Museum, becoming a focus for remembrance services there during the 1920s.

The train of Supreme Allied Commander Marshal Ferdinand Foch arrives at Compiègne on 6 November 1918 to finalise the terms of Germany's surrender with their representatives. After several days of talks, and dramatic developments elsewhere with the abdication of the Kaiser, it was clear that Germany was in no position to negotiate. It had to accept the Allied terms. The ceasefire was finally signed at 5am on 11 November 1918 and came into effect at 11am that day.

THE FIRST ARMISTICE DAY COMMEMORATION

The fervour of the summer event gave way to the first anniversary of the Armistice in the winter of 1919. The mood shifted from celebration to solemnity. On 11 November that year the Royal Family and politicians, along with Britain's military and religious leaders, gathered at the wooden Cenotaph for a service to pay tribute to the war dead. Services also took place at local war memorials across the country. The date became widely referred to as 'Armistice Day' in Britain and across the Empire. The same date was also marked in the USA, where it was known as 'Veterans' Day'.

The first anniversary also introduced an enduring ritual. The idea for a silent tribute to the First World War dead has been attributed to several people. One of those was Edward George Honey, an Australian journalist and veteran. He advocated the idea of communal silence in a letter to the London *Evening News* in May 1919:

> Five little minutes only. Five silent minutes of national remembrance. A very sacred intercession. Communion with the Glorious Dead who won us peace, and from the communion new strength, hope and faith in the morrow.

Church services, too, if you will, but in the street, the home, the theatre, anywhere, indeed, where Englishmen and their women chance to be, surely in this five minutes of bitter-sweet silence there will be service enough.

The suggestion caught hold. On 7 November 1919 George V approved the concept, but the length of the silence was restrained to two minutes. The moment of 11am was selected to reflect the precise time one year earlier when the Armistice had come into effect. The King issued a formal declaration:

To all my People.

Tuesday next, November 11, is the first anniversary of the Armistice which stayed the world-wide carnage of the four preceding years and marked the victory of right and freedom.

I believe that my people in every part of the Empire fervently wish to perpetuate the memory of that great deliverance and of those who laid down their lives to achieve it.

Above: 'Peace Day' celebrations in Dublin. Although London was the focus of 'Peace Day' events, crowds across the British Empire came out to celebrate. Thousands of Irish men had volunteered to serve in the conflict, many sensing an opportunity to gain political advantage for their conflicting aims. Nationalists sought a united Ireland while unionists wanted to retain the United Kingdom of Great Britain and Ireland.

Right: Sir Edwin Lutyens, seen here in 1924, was already a renowned architect when he was appointed one of three principal architects for the Imperial War Graves Commission. His secular style resulted in some of the most popular monuments to the British and Empire war dead, most notably the Cenotaph in London.

To afford an opportunity for the universal expression of this feeling it is my desire and hope that at the hour when the Armistice came into force – the eleventh hour of the eleventh day of the eleventh month – there may be for the brief space of two minutes a complete suspension of all our normal activities. During that time, except in the rare cases where this may be impracticable, all work, all sound, and all locomotion should cease, so that in perfect stillness the thoughts of everyone may be concentrated on reverent remembrance of the glorious dead.

No elaborate organisation appears to be necessary. At a given signal, which can easily be arranged to suit the circumstances of each locality, I believe that we shall all gladly interrupt our business and pleasure, whatever it may be, and unite in this simple service of silence and remembrance.

Not everyone was impressed. Writer Evelyn Waugh condemned the debut silence as 'a disgusting idea of artificial nonsense and sentimentality'. The *Manchester Guardian* reported a rather more consensual reaction in its vivid account of the first silence the following day:

The first stroke of eleven produced a magical effect. The tram cars glided into stillness, motors ceased to cough and fume, and stopped dead, and the mighty-limbed dray horses hunched back upon their loads and stopped also, seeming to do it of their own volition. Someone took off his hat, and with a nervous hesitancy the rest of the men bowed their heads also. Here and there an old soldier could be detected slipping unconsciously into the posture of 'attention'. An elderly woman, not far away, wiped her eyes, and the man beside her looked white and stern. Everyone stood very still ... The hush deepened. It had spread over the whole city and become so pronounced as to impress one with a sense of audibility. It was a silence which was almost pain ... And the spirit of memory brooded over it all.

CREATING THE CENOTAPH

The two minute silence went on to become – and remains – a firmly established annual ritual. Within days of its debut in 1919, Members of Parliament joined forces to demand that the wooden Cenotaph also become a fixed feature of Armistice Day anniversaries. Although misgivings were expressed over the Cenotaph's location, sandwiched between lanes of passing traffic on London's Whitehall, national newspapers campaigned for a permanent memorial to be built at the same site. Thousands of bereaved families had visited the wooden structure and men had doffed their caps to it as they walked past, an informal tribute that continued for many years. Lutyens designed an array of war memorials in Britain and across the Empire, including the imposing India Gate unveiled in New Dehli in 1921, while being deeply involved in the Imperial War Graves Commission's design planning for the cemeteries in its care. But it was the commission to make permanent the Cenotaph monument that cemented his reputation as the foremost figure in British remembrance architecture. Standing at over 10 metres (35 feet) high, his final design avoided complex embellishments.

The simplicity of the Cenotaph had a compelling lure. Along with the Unknown Warrior, this unfussy monument offered particular comfort to the families of the missing. It was a physical point at which individual grief converged with the national, imperial and Allied collective loss. The Cenotaph was not buttressed by religion. Lutyens' deliberately pared-down design avoided any overt theological symbolism, following the secular conditions of its commission. The monument was inscribed with three words of searing simplicity: 'The Glorious Dead'. The wording was so open that the Cenotaph later became – and remains – a focal point for remembrance of the British, Empire and Commonwealth war dead in conflicts that followed the First World War.

The most enduring cornerstones of British state remembrance came together on Armistice Day in 1920. The combination of a two minute silence, the new stone Cenotaph and a march past by representatives of ex-servicemen's associations and civilian organisations, as well as religious services, had a captivating alchemy. The gravity of the occasion was further heightened by the burial of the Unknown Warrior – the body of an unidentified British serviceman selected in France – in Westminster Abbey. After the ceremony at the Cenotaph a procession led by the king, the prime minister and military leaders travelled the short distance to the Abbey for the interment of the Unknown Warrior's body.

As with the year before, huge crowds flocked to London. From Armistice Day on Thursday 11 November 1920 to the following Monday morning, it was estimated that between 1 to 1.5 million people visited the stone Cenotaph. *The Times* reported continuing 'processions of people'.

The format of the formalities was replicated across the country as the years went by. Lutyens' Cenotaph design was even copied at varying scales in multiple locations, from Holyhead in Wales to Toronto in Canada. Its design had resonated quickly and deeply with the public, and continues to do so today.

From Mr. E. L. LUTYENS, A.R.A.

Telephone No. 95 Gerrard.
Telegraphic Address:
" Aedificavi, Vic, London."

17, QUEEN ANNE'S GATE,
WESTMINSTER, S.W.

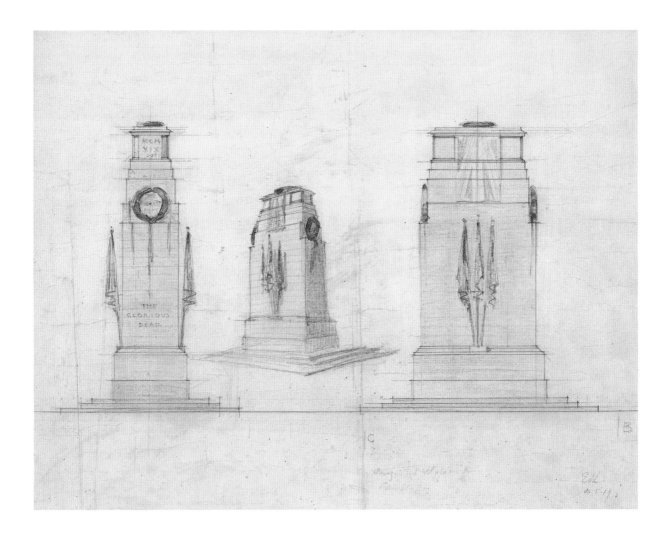

REMEMBRANCE FOR NATION AND EMPIRE

The extent to which religion should feature in the state's architectural approach to remembrance had stalked Luytens in other elements of his contracted work, most especially that for the Imperial War Graves Commission. His instructions on this latest assignment, from the Prime Minister David Lloyd George, were unequivocal: the Cenotaph had to be secular. Lloyd George laid down a firm line that a monument designed to reflect the tremendous loss of life suffered by the diverse Empire would not sit happily under a Christian facade, given the many non-Christian servicemen who had died.

The decision was received reproachfully in some quarters. But the popularity of the monument ran parallel to the difficulties that all religions found in explaining the scale of death. At home religious leaders found it impossible to provide solace through normal channels, such as funerals, while on the fighting fronts a crisis of faith was also felt. Signaller Stapleton Eachus recorded in his diary in September 1916 that 'Christ in my quarters is not believed in and a future life positively ridiculed'.

This was an impression further reinforced by what Reverend Ernest Crosse, an army chaplain, observed at the front:

> The real discovery chaplains made was not that there were so many varieties of Christianity, but that our ordinary exposition of it was too much divorced from the everyday things of life; with the result that most men had come to think of religion as something which only concerned certain parts of their life.

Concessions were made that undermined the state's secular approach to the Cenotaph's design. Religious elements were incorporated into the formal Armistice service held beside the monument, ranging from the singing of hymns to the raising of a large Christian cross. Despite this, the decisions made about national remembrance greatly, though far from completely, untethered state remembrance from religion.

The Cenotaph morphed into a memorial to the British and Empire dead, having initially started life as a tribute to the Allied dead. It was hoped that the democratic and oblique qualities of the two minute silence and the Cenotaph's blank canvas would unite people in memory of those who had died with a sense of shared national and imperial belonging. In 1923 *The Times* reported that:

> The Silence was poignant, the service was beautiful in its simplicity; but it was the tramp of the interminable legions of the bereaved, hour after hour, which brought realisation in the fullest measure of what the Cenotaph means to the common people.

The imperial dimension to state-sanctioned remembrance was an acute consideration. To the three-quarters of a million men from England, Scotland, Wales and Ireland who had lost their lives were joined approximately 72,000 Indian service personnel, 62,000 Australians, 12,000 South Africans, 60,000 Canadians, 18,000 New Zealanders, 1,200 Newfoundland soldiers and over 1,200 men from the Caribbean islands. These men had travelled across oceans and thousands of miles to fight for a country that most had never set foot in.

Attempts were made to memorialise the Empire war dead, in the places they hailed from and the locations where they had fatally fought. The dramatic Vimy Memorial in France was unveiled in France in 1936 to commemorate more than 11,000 missing men from the Canadian

Expeditionary Force who had no known grave. A memorial inspired by Indian architecture at Neuve Chapelle was created in the memory of over 4,700 Indian servicemen who died and whose resting places were never identified on the Western Front. These sites were chosen for their representative relevance to the fallen: many of the Canadian missing had died during the Battle of Vimy Ridge in 1917 while the Indian Corps fought its first major action as a cohesive unit at Neuve Chapelle in 1915. In the city of Canberra in Australia a complex of memorials, gardens and a museum were conceived as a permanent memorial to the country's war dead. After a slow beginning beset by fundraising problems, the Australian War Memorial opened on Remembrance Day 1941. As with so many of the imperial monuments, its terms were soon expanded to encompass the roll call of fatalities of the ongoing Second World War.

Attempts to correct or reinforce the recognition of imperial forces have continued into the twenty-first century. But the inconsistency of tributes to the Empire war dead was, and remains, subject to intense criticism. Labourers who died were given far less tangible recognition through memorials and medals than soldiers were. The Memorial Gates officially inaugurated in 2002 in London by Queen Elizabeth II are a

The Canadian Memorial at Vimy Ridge, dedicated to members of the Canadian Expeditionary Force killed during the First World War. Many of those commemorated died on surrounding land during the Battle of Vimy Ridge in 1917.

memorial to honour the 5 million men and women from the Indian subcontinent, Africa and the Caribbean who served with the armed forces in both the First and Second World Wars. But, for example, it took until 2017 for a memorial to be built in Britain that specifically commemorated the wartime contributions of its African and Caribbean colonies. The idea was conceived by the Nubian Jak Trust, a UK-based community organisation, to recognise the efforts of those who came from these areas to serve in Britain's forces, and those who died in doing so. The memorial is situated in London's Brixton, where many Caribbean families emigrated after the Second World War.

Britain faced an acute problem in dealing with the commemoration of its Irish forces. Fractious nationalist and unionist sentiment had led the United Kingdom of Great Britain and Ireland to the brink of a civil war shortly before the First World War broke out. The world war presented an opportunity to both persuasions; each believed that vital influence could be gained by serving. Nearly 50,000 Irishmen died during the war from both sides of the political – and often religious – divide. Following the Irish War of Independence, 26 of Ireland's 32 counties were granted the status of a self-governing dominion – the Irish Free State – within the British Empire in 1921. The subsequent civil war over the agreement to leave six Ulster counties as part of the United Kingdom saw attentions further drift away from commemorating the world war's human cost, in which both Catholic nationalists and Protestant unionists had invested so many hopes.

A prominent city centre tribute to the Irish war dead in the country's capital, Dublin, was emphatically ruled out. Kevin O'Higgins, the Minister for Justice, had himself lost a brother in the First World War. He starkly laid bare the nationalist commemoration conundrum in 1927:

> No one denies the patriotic motives which induced the vast majority of those [Irish] men to join the British army to take part in the Great War, and yet it is not on their sacrifice that this State is based, and I have no desire to see it suggested that it is.

The following year Marshal Ferdinand Foch – the French commander in chief – led a warm tribute to the Irish contribution to Allied victory, in which he felt compelled to express that 'I saw Irishmen of the North and the South forget their age-long differences and fight side by side, giving their lives freely for the common cause'. Foch insisted that:

> The heroic dead of Ireland have every right to the homage of the living; for they proved in some of the heaviest fighting of the world war that the

Left: Sir Edward Carson, leader of the Irish Unionist Party, inspects members of the Ulster Volunteer Force (UVF) prior to the outbreak of the First World War. The UVF was founded in 1913, when Ireland was on the brink of civil war. It sought to resist the implementation of Home Rule, which would allow Ireland to govern elements of its own affairs independently from the British Empire.

Right: The Irish National War Memorial Gardens at Islandbridge on the outskirts of Dublin. They were designed by Sir Edwin Lutyens to commemorate almost 50,000 Irishmen who died during the First World War.

unconquerable spirit of the Irish race, the spirit that has placed them among the world's greatest soldiers, still lives and is stronger than ever it was.

Eventually Sir Edwin Lutyens was once again enrolled to design a tribute to all Irishmen who died as a result of the First World War while fighting for the British Empire. The War Memorial Gardens by the banks of the River Liffey in Dublin were only completed in the late 1930s, long after the end of the First World War and Ireland's subsequent violent assertion of nationhood. Although thoughtful and grand, the gardens were never intended to provide a central civic focus as the Cenotaph in London did, situated, as they were, miles from the city centre. The sectarian violence that beset Northern Ireland in the late twentieth century further contributed to a widespread dislocation from the memory of Irish losses in the First World War. But a resurgence of interest followed the advances made towards peace in the late 1990s.

National identity was a huge issue within mainland Britain too, albeit less fraught with violence. It further blurred the remit of state remembrance. An official Welsh National War Memorial was unveiled in Cardiff in 1928, long before the city became the capital of Wales in the 1950s. It commemorated the 35,000 'sons of Wales who gave their lives for their country in the war of 1914–1918'. Funds for the memorial were raised through public subscription. The official decision – made in 1923 after years of debate – to forge ahead with the construction of a memorial for the Scottish war dead at Edinburgh Castle reflected the persistent complexity of identity within the United Kingdom. Arguments raged over whether it was necessary for a country without its own government to assert national identity within a political union – which in itself had to represent an entire global Empire in its remembrance. These debates were exuberantly explained by the 8th Duke of Atholl – a veteran of the war and the chief instigator of the Scottish memorial campaign – in 1920:

> I am afraid that all the rebel spirit that lies dormant in every Scot roused itself within me, and I made a public statement that if the people of Scotland wished to have a National War Memorial to commemorate their own dead it would not be in Hyde Park, London, and put up with Government money, but it would be put up by Scottish hands, with Scottish money, on Scottish soil.

These instincts were further complicated by the local war memorial rush that was in full swing and by tensions between Scotland's capital, Edinburgh, and its largest city, Glasgow, over the location of any national memorial. A successful fundraising drive among Scottish residents and diaspora gave the national memorial's claim to popular support an authentic basis. By 1927 arguments about its form were finally settled with the opening of a Hall of Honour and Shrine, designed by Sir Robert Lorimer, at Edinburgh Castle. The names of the Scottish war dead from the First World War were contained in Rolls of Honour, while the memorial also paid visual tribute to the contribution of the home front. The vivid memorial was a stark contrast to the deliberate blank canvas of the London Cenotaph. It tapped into a sense of identity that unionists such as Atholl believed existed independently of the United Kingdom and local community. Being Scottish manifested in feeling oneself to be such, rather than by satisfying a strictly defined set of criteria. But being officially declared 'Scottish' for the purposes of inclusion in the Rolls of Honour did depend on a deceased person being:

> A member of the Armed Forces of the Crown or of the Merchant Navy who was either a Scotsman (i.e. born in Scotland or who had a Scottish-born father or mother) or served in a Scottish Regiment and was killed or died (except as a result of suicide) as a result of a wound, injury or disease sustained (a) in a theatre of operations for which a medal has been or is awarded; or (b) whilst on duty in aid of the Civil Power.

REMEMBRANCE OVER THE YEARS

The issue of state remembrance became thornier still as the First World War spectacularly failed to be 'the war to end all wars'. The forms of remembrance carved out in the 1920s were retained and expanded, rather than overhauled, after the devastating Second World War. Wreath laying, the service at the Cenotaph and march-pasts persisted as ways to commemorate men and women who died in that war. The most significant change came in 1939, several months into the Second World War, with the move away from strict observation of 11 November on Armistice Day to 'Remembrance Sunday' on the Sunday nearest to that date. Wholesale changes to the format of the day's commemoration have been avoided by British governments over the decades, with the First World War traditions showing their staying power.

Veterans perceived the state's approach to remembrance in many ways. One veteran, Trooper George Jameson of the Royal Horse Artillery, responded very positively to what he experienced:

> When I was working in London, I was in St Stephen's House for a spell. And I rang Elsie up and said, 'Come into London – we can nip around from St Stephen's House to the Cenotaph for the Armistice Day service.' We came through Scotland Yard and came right opposite the Cenotaph with the whole place packed, and just stood at the back. All we could really do was listen, we couldn't see very much. The thing that impressed me most about it was the two minute silence. It was terrific. I've never heard silence pulsate to that extent. There was no doubt about it – the human emotion that must have been pent up in that massive crowd seemed to vibrate in the air and you were conscious of it. It was terrific and I said to Elsie, 'Did that get you like that?' She said, 'Yes – it was terrific wasn't it?' I said, 'I never would have believed it possible that a crowd of people like that, packing Whitehall from end to end, suddenly silenced for two minutes' – that impressed me very much.

However, the general public were not universally supportive or moved. *The Times* reported of the 1921 Armistice Day that 'a crowd of extremists beat time with their feet and sang revolutionary songs' during the two minute silence in Liverpool. Another such incident was recorded in Dundee on the same day, with a newspaper reporting that 'when the Silence began the Communists created a great disturbance, shouting, singing, and resorting to all kinds of expedients to cause noise... Many of them had carried the red flag and other banners, and these were wrested from them, torn up, and cast upon the street'. Veterans were

A member of the public records the formalities taking place at London's Cenotaph on Remembrance Sunday in November 2017.

occasionally part of the disturbance. In 1937 Stanley Storey, a veteran with mental health issues, interrupted the silence in London with the cry of 'hypocrites!' He was quickly detained by police as a threat to the king's safety. It made front page news the next day. The date has also incited, on occasion, attack. On Remembrance Sunday in 1987 an Irish Republican Army (IRA) bomb was detonated at a service at the local war memorial in Enniskillen in County Fermanagh, attended by hundreds of people; 11 civilians were killed. A twelfth man died 13 years later from injuries sustained that day.

More universally, in the 1920s, there was a constant tension between solemnity and celebration on Armistice Day. For many the date represented survival and victory, where the desire to celebrate was natural. This was alluded to in 1925 by none other than Earl Haig, formerly the most senior commander of British forces:

> I recommend that Armistice Day be observed throughout the Empire as a day of Remembrance... In the evening people should rejoice according to taste.

For the profoundly grief-stricken, the day painfully ruptured an aching emotional wound each year. But most bereaved families, and society at large, took the idea of an annual routine in which the war dead were remembered to their hearts.

One hundred years after the First World War ended, the ways in which the British government shaped remembrance on behalf of the nation remain fixed points in the state calendar. The facets of national remembrance have become almost as recognisable as the events and deaths they were established to commemorate. Rituals and monuments remain crucial conduits for state remembrance of the unsurpassed death toll for Britain's forces in the First World War. But a sense of identity, within tangled political and imperial structures, was complex and debates over remembrance at this level reflected many tensions. The ceremonial aspects of British state remembrance joined forces with the poppy, arguably the most potent symbol of First World War remembrance. This simple flower motif was not the imposition of the state, although it made regular appearances in national rituals. It was worn then, and is worn now, by some of the most prominent figures in public life. The wearing of a red fabric or paper poppy acquired astounding popular momentum in the years after the war, and has become a lasting expression of remembrance.

8

THE REMEMBRANCE POPPY

The red poppy has arguably become the most enduring icon of remembrance of the First World War – an instantly recognisable symbol linked to the grave human cost of the conflict. That it became so was the result of a botanical phenomenon – a shocking burst of colourful plant life in otherwise unrelentingly bleak landscapes on the war's fighting fronts. Modern weaponry pulverised both soil and men in unprecedented waves of destruction. Yet the high-explosive shells that tore into the earth had a surprising generative effect. Inadvertently they created the perfect conditions in which a simple, translucent red flower could grow – *Papaver Rhoeas*, the red corn poppy.

The savage violence stirred the ground so effectively that millions of tall, slender poppy stalks flourished on the Western Front. Though it appeared so delicate and incongruous, this short-lived, crimson wild flower, which could reach over 75 cm (30 inches) in height, was actually rather robust. The annual plant thrived in fertile, well-drained soils such as chalk, which made up the Somme battlefield in 1916. As the summer sun beat down, the poppies put on an expansive and extravagant display, becoming indelibly connected with the destruction that took place all around them.

During the war, many soldiers plucked and pressed the fragile heads of the corn poppy into letters home as a floral greeting. The petals gave a cheerful flash of colour in a drab world of khaki and mud. Other flowers also grew in parts of the Western Front, their beauty relished by men surrounded by landscapes of devastation. Reginald Bryan recalled his delight at encountering wild flowers in springtime, evidence of a natural world amidst the destruction of conflict:

> One afternoon at the end of April I went to a wood which had been destroyed by guns and had the surprise of my life. The trees had without exception been splintered to smithereens and the ground was strewed with wreckage and broken branches, but I also found that the wood was covered with a mass of yellow wild-flowers, oxslips and cowslips! Elsewhere there was not a sign of a flower but here they were growing in thousands. I was delighted with my find and gathered some and sent a box of them home to Mother.

Yet it was the poppy that captured the imagination of contemporaries to become the most evocative symbol of remembrance. Its formidable power was harnessed by soldier poets.

'IN FLANDERS FIELDS'

One of the war's most famous poems about the flower had its roots in the bloody spring of 1915, as the war entered a grinding deadlock. The Second

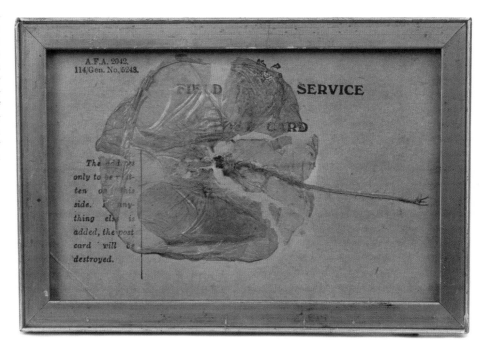

Battle of Ypres was one of many failed attempts to break the stalemate. Canadian physician Lieutenant Colonel John McCrae worked in a dressing station extremely close to the front line; here, embedded with frontline soldiers, he could quickly tend to wounds sustained in the fighting. McCrae was no stranger to the battlefield. He had fought in the Boer Wars in South Africa at the turn of the century before returning across the Atlantic, very much by choice, to serve in the forces of the British Empire once more during the First World War.

Like most of the soldier poets who became famous after the conflict, McCrae was not an established writer. He had poems published in his university newspaper in Montreal, but poetry was no more than a pastime. As a military doctor, he used snatched moments to pen verse in response to what he experienced and saw, as did other soldier poets. Like millions more, McCrae also corresponded with home. In a letter to his mother written during the Second Battle of Ypres in late April, the 42-year-old described the scene around him:

> Traffic whizzed by – ambulances, transport, ammunition, supplies, despatch riders – and the shells thundered into the town, or burst high in the air nearer us, and the refugees streamed. Women, old men, little children, hopeless, tearful, quiet or excited, tired, dodging the traffic, – and the wounded in singles or in groups. Here and there I could give a momentary help, and the ambulances picked up as they could. So

the cold moonlight night wore on – no change save that the towers of Ypres showed up against the glare of the city burning; and the shells still sailed in.

Early in May 1915, in a break from tending to the wounded and dying, McCrae wrote a new poem. The poppies that grew in abundance in the expanding 'Essex Farm' cemetery nearby were his inspiration. The poem, most commonly known as 'In Flanders Fields', also came off the back of the death of a close friend in action. Its very first iteration read:

In Flanders fields the poppies grow
Between the crosses, row on row,
That mark our place: and in the sky
The larks, still bravely singing, fly
Scarce heard amid the guns below.

We are the dead. Short days ago
We lived, felt dawn, saw sunset glow,
Loved and were loved, and now we lie
In Flanders fields.

Take up our quarrel with the foe;
To you from failing hands we throw
The torch; be yours to hold it high,
If ye break faith with us who die
We shall not sleep, though poppies grow
In Flanders fields.

McCrae's later tweaks saw words such as 'grow' in the first line become 'blow'. The poppy had now become laden with weighty symbolism. For some the blooms served as a hopeful beacon of life in the midst of death; conversely its colour reminded others of a brutal blood sacrifice. McCrae himself associated the profligate wild flowers with the spiralling tally of war fatalities. Whatever people saw in the poppy, it almost always went beyond its humble botanical status as a rampant weed.

McCrae did not keep his poem private. Later in the year he sent the piece off to *Punch*, a hugely popular satirical magazine, and the verses first appeared in print on 8 December 1915. McCrae's work seized the imagination of soldiers and civilians alike. In a contextual essay about McCrae's life, written to accompany an edition of his poetry printed in 1919, his friend Sir Andrew Macphail described the widespread affection for the poem:

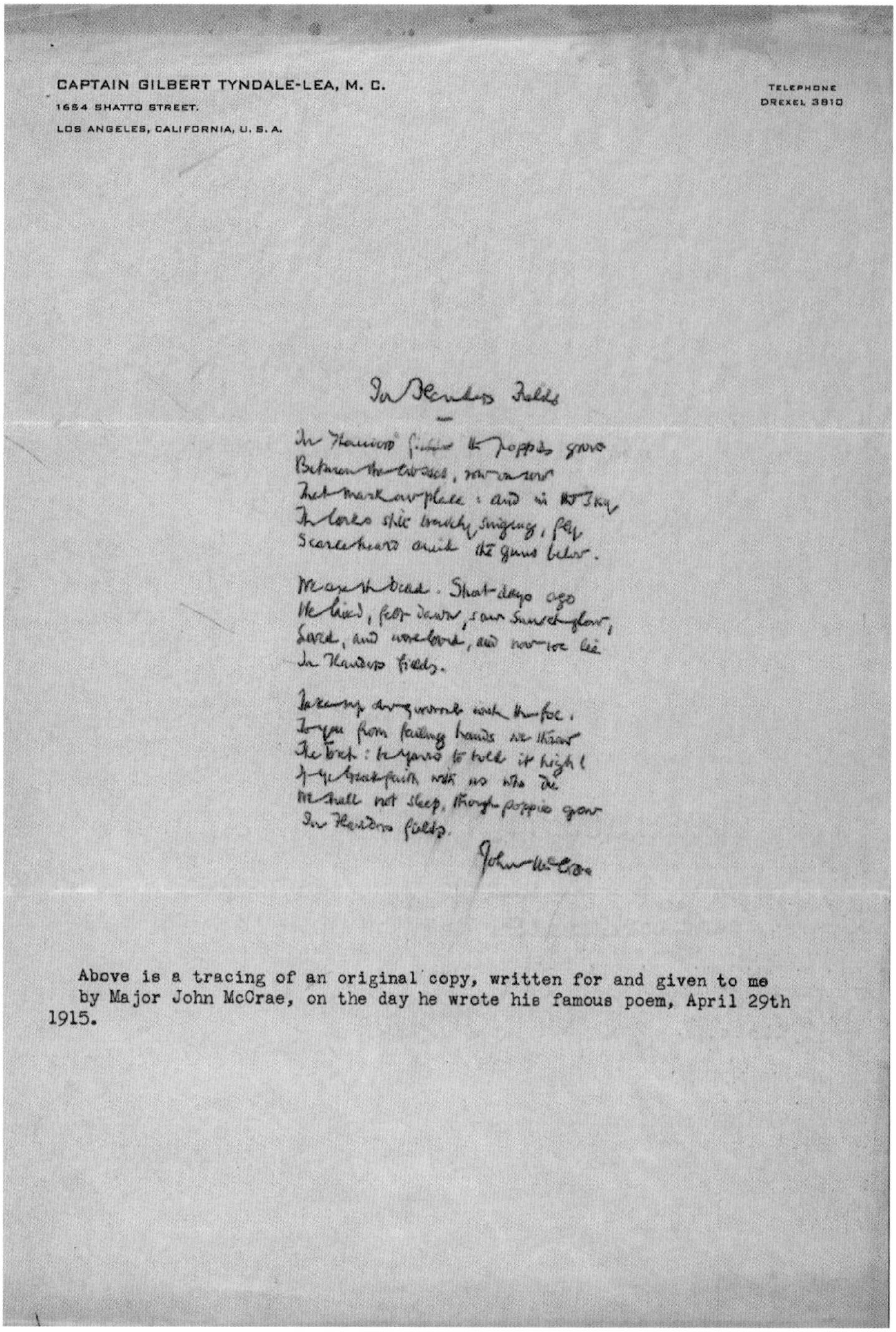

A tracing of an original holograph copy of John McCrae's poem 'In Flanders Fields'. It was given to Captain Gilbert Tyndale-Lea by McCrae on 29 April 1915 – the day he wrote the poem during a break from treating the wounded. McCrae later changed the word 'grow' in the first line seen here to 'blow'.

It circulates, as a song should circulate, by the living word of mouth, not by printed characters. That is the true test of poetry, – its insistence on making itself learnt by heart.

McCrae's war experiences did not end there, although he never worked so close to the front line after 1915. He had senior postings in a major military hospital behind the lines near Boulogne in France. The strain weakened him, according to Macphail, and he died from the rapid onset of double pneumonia and cerebral infection in January 1918:

> After his experience at the front the old gaiety never returned. There were moments of irascibility and moods of irritation. The desire for solitude grew upon him, and with Bonfire and Bonneau [McCrae's dogs] he would go apart for long afternoons far afield by the roads and lanes about Boulogne. The truth is: he felt that he and all had failed, and that the torch was thrown from failing hands. We have heard much of the suffering, the misery, the cold, the wet, the gloom of those first three winters; but no tongue has yet uttered the inner misery of heart that was bred of those three years of failure to break the enemy's force.

KEEPING THE FAITH

John McCrae never lived to see the full impact of his poem on the flower it took its inspiration from. The poppy's status as an instantly recognisable remembrance symbol and fundraising icon began after his lifetime. Two days before the fighting ended, a 49-year-old American academic from the University of Georgia stumbled across a reprinting of McCrae's poem. Moina Michael had left a teaching post to work for the Young Women's Christian Association (YWCA) Overseas War Secretaries (OWS). During a conference in New York City on 9 November 1918, she took a moment to flick through a copy of the *Ladies' Home Journal*. A reprint of McCrae's poem caught her attention.

In her memoirs Michael described reading the poem and her response as a 'full spiritual experience'. Within minutes she had hurriedly penned her own poem in direct response to McCrae's lines. Her creation, 'We Shall Keep the Faith', read:

> Oh! You who sleep in Flanders' fields,
> Sleep sweet – to rise anew,
> We caught the torch you threw,
> And holding head high we kept
> The faith with those that died.
>
> We cherish too, the poppy red,
> That grows on fields where valor led.

It seems to signal the skies
That blood of heroes never dies,
But lends a lustre to the red
Of the flower that blooms above the dead
In Flanders' fields,

And now the torch and poppy red
Wear in honour of the dead.
Fear not that ye have died for naught
We've learned the lesson that ye taught,
In Flanders' fields.

For Moina Michael the poppy was a symbolic link between the living and the dead. Two days after the New York conference she decided to make the link tangible. She purchased 25 artificial flowers in a nearby department store, armed with cash donated by delegates on 11 November 1918. The fighting had just ended with a ceasefire. Upon Michael's return, attendees of the conference enthusiastically pinned the flowers to their lapels. The symbolic power of the poppy grew vociferously after the violence ended and Michael enthusiastically promoted her vision for the flower. Her efforts were beset by difficulties, but she pushed on, fervently advocating the adoption of the poppy far and wide. In 1920 the American Legion, a major veterans' organisation, formally approved the poppy as its symbol for remembering the war dead. In the autumn of 1921 the Legion abandoned its use of the poppy by flitting to the daisy, before embracing the poppy once again a year later in 1922. However, its initial embrace of the red flower was instrumental in the poppy's transatlantic success.

The poppy might never have been adopted as a symbol of remembrance in Britain were it not for the efforts of a woman from war-ravaged France. Already known as the 'Poppy Lady of France', Anna Guérin had organised a network of French war widows who made artificial poppy flowers from silk which Guérin arranged to have distributed and sold abroad. Guérin energetically organised 'Poppy Days' across the United States of America in 1920. The funds raised went towards local causes for disabled veterans or those in financial hardship while her charity for war-orphaned children in France, La Ligue Americaine Francaise des Enfants, received a share of the proceeds. Guérin's vociferous networking across the Atlantic was deeply influential in persuading the American Legion to adopt the red poppy as its remembrance symbol at national level. She also advocated for the poppy to become a fundraising symbol in Canada, New Zealand and Australia.

THE POWER OF THE POPPY

In August 1921 Britain became the focus of Anna Guérin's next campaign. She arrived in London, bringing her vehement energy to the door of the newly formed British Legion. The organisation was a conglomeration of former veterans' associations with a fundraising arm; it had the personal patronage of Britain's most senior commander during the war, Earl Haig. The idea for the red poppy as a remembrance symbol and fundraising spur moved him greatly and he personally endorsed the campaign. Haig's reputation was in its zenith, despite the enormous loss of life that occurred under his command and which was to tarnish his reputation in later reappraisals of his career. In the 1920s it was widely perceived that Haig's leadership had vitally contributed to the Allied victory over Germany. His support was a great asset to the early poppy campaign.

Guérin persuaded the British Legion to order a vast tranche of the silk poppies made by French war widows, with a percentage of the funds raised to be set aside for her own work in France. The Legion needed to raise essential funds for its own ambitions to support British veterans in peacetime so – despite reservations about whether the idea would catch on – 9 million poppies were ordered. The first 'Poppy Day' was held on 11 November 1921. The British Legion had decided to capitalise on the way in which Armistice Day had already become a fixture of significance in the national calendar.

Volunteers were rallied across the country; a huge logistical effort. Each wore a tray full of the silk flowers to sell in the streets and public areas. People were asked to make a donation of whatever they could afford in return for a poppy, at no fixed price. Buying and wearing a poppy was a voluntary, personal endeavour. The power of the appeal was glaringly obvious from the start; sellers could not keep up with demand. It was a runaway success, raising over £3 million in 2018 terms.

The French silk flowers were handed over along with a leaflet containing both Canadian John McCrae's poem and American Moina Michael's response to it, drawing together all of the threads that had brought the poppy to British shores. The flower became deeply associated with the loss of life in the war as much as with those who had survived it and required assistance with their ongoing troubles.

Given this triumph, in order to ensure an adequate and ambitious supply of poppies and to direct all donations to British veterans, the British Legion made the decision to abandon Anna Guérin's silk poppies. Instead, it set up a bespoke artificial poppy factory to provide employment directly to wounded ex-servicemen. This was the brainchild of Major George Howson. There were concerns that Britain should be fundraising solely for its own needy as a priority, whatever the humanitarian needs in former Allied countries.

A British artificial fabric poppy from an early Poppy Appeal. A tag attached to the poppy bears the inscription 'EARL HAIG'S APPEAL For Ex-Service Men of all Ranks and their Dependents BRITISH LEGION 'REMEMBRANCE DAY'.

The demand for poppies in the south was so high in the early appeals that Scotland was not properly supplied with remembrance poppies, despite the country having suffered in the region of 100,000 deaths attributable to the war. Earl Haig's connections with Scotland were also plentiful; he was born in Edinburgh and buried in the Scottish Borders following his death in 1928. His wife Dorothy, Countess Haig, fronted a push to set up an exclusive production line for Scotland. The Lady Haig Poppy Factory was established in Edinburgh in 1926 to do just that. The poppies sold north of the border differed by having four petals and no green leaf – a design revision attributed to this day to the belief that the English version's greenery was both 'botanically incorrect' and an unnecessary production cost that diverted funds from the needy. Britain's poppy factories soon branched out, as the flowers were incorporated into the ceremonial aspects of the new Armistice Day formalities. Wreaths were produced for individuals and associations to place a more substantial floral tribute on war graves, at local war memorials or upon major war memorials such as the Cenotaph.

Volunteer poppy sellers were integral to the success of the appeals. This was recognised by Earl Haig in his capacity as President of the British Legion. In a widely reproduced letter of thanks, he warmly acknowledged the army of sellers:

Field Marshal Sir Douglas Haig, who commanded the British Expeditionary Force in France and Belgium from December 1915 until the end of the war. Haig's legacy has been hotly contested in recent years, notably regarding his rationale for the campaigns in which hundreds of thousands of British soldiers under his command died. In the 1920s Haig devoted himself to the care of ex-servicemen in need and lent his name to the fundraising of voluntary donations through the sale of artificial poppies.

A lapel badge worn by members of the British Legion, which was formed in 1920 from an amalgamation of three ex-servicemen's organisations: the Comrades of the Great War, the National Association of Discharged Sailors and Soldiers and the National Federation of Discharged and Demobilised Sailors and Soldiers. The organisation became known as the Royal British Legion in 1971.

As the Poppy symbolises the sacrifice of those who laid down their lives, so your kindly help for those gallant survivors who are now in want, typifies that spirit of gratitude and service, which is beyond all praise or earthly reward.

CHALLENGES TO THE POPPY

It is impossible to gauge whether John McCrae could ever have imagined the connection between his poem's poppies and the status they would acquire in Britain as the foremost symbol of the war's human cost. The tradition of wearing poppies allowed an individual tribute to become part of a collective movement to ensure remembrance of the First World War. Artificial poppies continue to be sold in Britain and parts of its former Empire to raise money for veterans in need, and to remember those who lost their lives in the First World War and subsequent conflicts. But the poppy and the politics around it have become complex in more recent times, especially as new conflicts have arisen.

Alternative poppies were a reaction to diverging attitudes about the conflict and overlooked contributions to the war effort. They included black poppies to remember the lives lost by non-white servicemen and purple poppies to honour animals killed. White poppies were, and remain, the most familiar alternative poppy. They were first sold by the social justice movement the Co-operative Women's Guild in 1933, with the Peace Pledge Union (PPU) taking over in 1934. The white poppy's meaning was and remains stridently anti-war. The wearing of a PPU flower had three main aims: to remember all the victims of war, both military and civilian, to stand up for peace and to challenge militarism, reflecting the belief that 'working for peace is the natural consequence of remembering the victims of war'.

The red poppy itself has been subject to disputes and appropriations, more recently by far-right organisations. As early as the 1920s the matter of other groups selling 'competing' red poppies had become a concern to the House of Commons. Brighton MP Sir Cooper Rawson pushed for a law preventing the import and sale of German-manufactured red poppies that had been making their way into Britain in 1928. He considered moral outrage

Poppy wreaths are laid at the base of the Cenotaph in London during the interwar period. Artificial poppies ranged from the simple lapel variant to elaborate wreaths laid by veterans' associations or senior royal, political and military figures at Armistice services. Today the Royal British Legion's fundraising poppy range includes jewellery and clothing.

the appropriate response towards anyone guilty of producing 'rival' poppies in Britain itself, deceitfully diverting funds from the British Legion's work:

> Unfortunately, there are in this country at the present time, I am ashamed to say, people who are manufacturing, for profit, British Legion poppies in competition with the British Legion official poppy. These are being manufactured, distributed, and sold merely to undercut the British Legion official poppy. ... I think we shall have to leave it to the discerning British public to find them out and when they have found them out to expose them.

The present day (now Royal) British Legion lays out its belief in its poppies as 'a symbol of Remembrance and hope' inspired by the natural colour of field poppies. The Legion is adamant that their fundraising flower is not 'a symbol of death or a sign of support for war' nor 'a reflection of politics or religion'. Nor are the artificial creations red 'to reflect the colour of blood'. Instead, in 2018, the Royal British Legion believes that:

> Wearing a poppy is a personal choice and reflects individual and personal memories. It is not compulsory but is greatly appreciated by those it helps – our beneficiaries: those currently serving in our Armed Forces, veterans, and their families and dependants.

The remembrance poppy's literal and symbolic seeds were rooted in the war's turbulent landscapes. And it was also from the battlefield that soldiers collected and brought home man-made souvenirs of their experiences, from shell cases to enemy equipment. Official policy was quick to follow their lead, with a formal endeavour to retrieve and display significant objects and fragments from the field of conflict. The foundation of the Imperial War Museum for this purpose, and its ambition to develop collective understanding of the experience of war, was joined by wider cultural remembrance. Art, poems, literature, stage productions, films and music came to express or imagine the First World War's human impact. Some of these works harnessed the symbol of the poppy, none more so than the art installation at the Tower of London that proved so compelling in 2014. The major art installation *Blood Swept Lands and Seas of Red* marked the centenary of the start of the First World War, featuring nearly 900,000 ceramic poppies individually affixed into the ground within the Tower's dry moat. Over the last 100 years, a deluge of cultural outpourings have created a powerful tapestry of informal, creative remembrance.

9

CULTURAL
REMEMBRANCE

The First World War unleashed a torrent of creativity in response to its devastating scale of death. From best-selling literature to award-winning popular films, the First World War has been imaginatively conceived by writers, poets, film-makers, musicians and artists through the decades. Some of this material was created by people who had personally experienced the very action their works portrayed. Others were inspired by events long after their conclusion, telling inventive 'war stories' in print, on the stage, through music, in the cinema and on television were discovered. Over the past century readers and audiences have been gifted a trove of characters, scenes and tunes through which to engage with the conflict. For many the consumption of these cultural offerings has become in itself an act of remembrance. The creation of a major museum to collect and display objects from the war further expanded the ways of confronting the war's human impact, its death toll and its searing emotional legacy.

Previous page: One of the Imperial War Museum's art galleries at the Crystal Palace in May 1921, with John Singer Sargent's imposing painting *Gassed* displayed on the left-hand wall. The museum's collections encompass art, weapons, uniforms, letters, diaries, film, photographs and much more.

SOLDIER POETS OF THE FIRST WORLD WAR

John McCrae, author of the poem 'In Flanders Fields', was one of a host of soldier poets who penned impressions of the war, based on their own experiences. The poets' creative momentum was fuelled by the ongoing conflict. Many of them found posthumous fame once the war was over and their own lives had been lost. The most popular poetry written and read during the war was often jingoistic, supportive of the war or romantic. Rupert Brooke died from illness during his service. His best-known war poem, 'The Soldier', imagined the thoughts of a soldier waiting to go into battle:

> If I should die, think only this of me:
>   That there's some corner of a foreign field
> That is for ever England. There shall be
>   In that rich earth a richer dust concealed;
> A dust whom England bore, shaped, made aware,
>   Gave, once, her flowers to love, her ways to roam,
> A body of England's, breathing English air,
>   Washed by the rivers, blest by suns of home.
>
> And think, this heart, all evil shed away,
>   A pulse in the eternal mind, no less
>   Gives somewhere back the thoughts by England given;
> Her sights and sounds; dreams happy as her day;
>   And laughter, learnt of friends; and gentleness,
>   In hearts at peace, under an English heaven.

Wilfred Owen would become one of the most famous British war poets. Deployed to France in December 1916, he suffered so severely from 'shell shock' that he was sent back to Britain for treatment. His poetic endeavours were boosted by the friendship he struck up with fellow poet and in-patient Siegfried Sassoon at Craiglockhart War Hospital in Edinburgh. Owen's newly honed poetic voice described the bleak reality of life on the Western Front, and the shattering effects of violence upon human flesh. He went back into action in France in the war's final summer. On 4 November 1918, a week before the Armistice, he was killed.

Owen died without ever knowing fame or the impact his poetry would have, but his work profoundly shaped perceptions of the First World War. Both he and Sassoon questioned how the conflict could be justified in the face of so much suffering, despite both men being decorated for bravery. The final lines of Owen's poem 'Dulce Et Decorum Est' make this plain as they convey the devastating aftermath of an imagined gas attack:

> If in some smothering dreams you too could pace
> Behind the wagon that we flung him in,
> And watch the white eyes writhing in his face,
> His hanging face, like a devil's sick of sin;
> If you could hear, at every jolt, the blood
> Come gargling from the froth-corrupted lungs,
> Obscene as cancer, bitter as the cud
> Of vile, incurable sores on innocent tongues, –
> My friend, you would not tell with such high zest
> To children ardent for some desperate glory,
> The old Lie: Dulce et decorum est
> Pro patria mori.

As the 1920s wore on, sentiments about human suffering, incompetent leadership and purposelessness gained traction with readers. Sassoon's 1918 poem 'The General' resonated with readers seeking a censorious perspective, while expressing a deep empathy for the ordinary soldier:

> 'Good-morning; good-morning!' the General said
> When we met him last week on our way to the line.
> Now the soldiers he smiled at are most of 'em dead,
> And we're cursing his staff for incompetent swine.
> 'He's a cheery old card,' grunted Harry to Jack
> As they slogged up to Arras with rifle and pack.
>
> But he did for them both by his plan of attack.

Wilfred Owen became one of the most famous soldier poets of the First World War. His poems, including 'Dulce Et Decorum Est' and 'Anthem for Doomed Youth', described the violence and suffering inflicted upon the ordinary soldier. Owen never lived to see the impact his verse had on perceptions of the conflict, or how popular his work became; he was killed in action one week before the Armistice.

Such poems were embraced as an authentic expression of the war's brutal reality. Their collective body became a means by which the conflict was kept alive, most especially through their teaching in classrooms across Britain, and their reflection of a growing belief that so many had died for so little apparent purpose.

LITERATURE OF WAR

British authors were recruited as weapons in what was viewed as a war of minds as much as military might. The government enlisted the signatures of 53 well known writers – including Thomas Hardy and H G Wells – to an 'Authors' Declaration' in September 1914. It railed against

Germany's 'brute force'. Novels imbued with explicit or oblique support of the British war effort flew off the printing presses during the war. Household names included Arthur Conan Doyle and John Buchan, their stories and opinion-pieces forming part of the arsenal of an increasingly sophisticated British propaganda machine. In an age before domestic radio and long before television, the printed word was the chief means by which news and propaganda spread.

A decade after the fighting had ended, there was an eruption of war literature which took a very different tone. It centred on the plight of the ordinary soldier or protested against any sense that the war was worthy of the lives lost. The most compelling British book of this kind was Robert Graves' autobiography *Goodbye to All That*, published in 1929 and written deliberately to appeal to a public keen to embrace a sensational

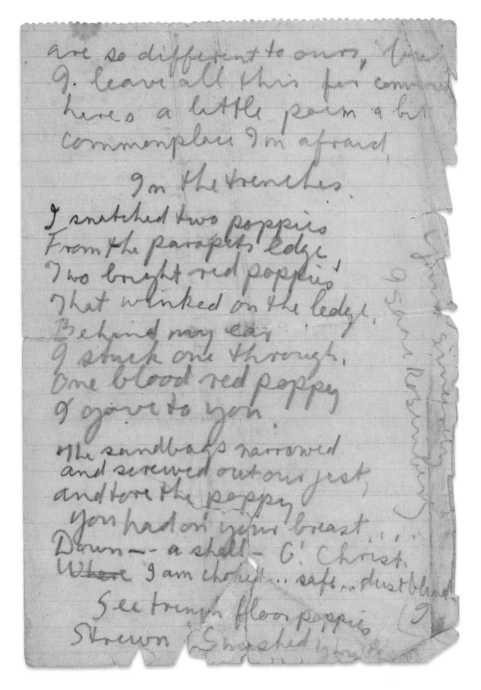

are so different to ours. Then
I leave all this for comrade
here's a little poem a bit
commonplace I'm afraid.

       In the trenches.

I snatched two poppies
From the parapet's ledge,
Two bright red poppies
That winked on the ledge.
Behind my ear
I stuck one through,
One blood red poppy
I gave to you.

The sandbags narrowed
and screwed out our jest,
and tore the poppy
You had on your breast . . .
Down — a shell — O! Christ,
Where I am choked . . . safe . . . dust blind
See trench floor poppies
Strewn. Smashed . . . .

account of the war. Graves' subversive description of his rush to join the
army to avoid university, his reliance on alcohol to steady his nerves at the
front and his disdain for British popular wartime opinion would probably
have been unacceptable to publishing houses during the war itself.

By the late 1920s readers were even challenged to empathise with the
former enemy. *All Quiet on the Western Front* epitomised this shift. Its

author, Erich Maria Remarque, had served as an infantryman, lending authority to his novel's desolate view of the war's appalling suffering. Its main character, Paul Baumer, joins the army with his German classmates, full of youthful vigour, only for their giddy optimism to be annihilated by the ravages of conflict. The book proved an immense publishing success, in both Germany and Allied countries alike, and a hugely popular film adaptation in English followed rapidly on its heels. The film touched upon a sense of ludicrousness over the war's origins; soldiers in one scene question the absurdity of a situation in which 'a mountain in Germany gets mad at a field over in France'. The story tapped into an escalating belief that violence itself was the real adversary, and that the Great War had to be 'the war to end all wars'. As a result, *All Quiet on the Western Front* was nominated for the Nobel Peace Prize in 1931. The nascent Nazis abhorred the work's sentiments and its failure to portray German soldiers as militaristic victors. After the National Socialists came to power in Germany in 1933, it became a crime to own a copy of the book.

In far more recent years, novels have continued to put humanity before nationality. Primary school teacher Michael Morpurgo drew inspiration from animals in *War Horse*, his 2007 children's novel. When war breaks out in 1914, a young farm horse called Joey is wrenched away from Albert, the teenager who raised him, having been sold to the army by Albert's father. Joey is thrust into action on the Western Front, mirroring the fact that the British Army used over one million horses and mules for transport during the war. Almost half of these animals were killed. Morpurgo reflected on his tale:

> It's about loss, it's about grief... but mostly about that war seen through the eyes of a horse which means that you can see it from [the] point of view of all the armies and indeed the people whose lands are being fought over ... so it's seen through the eyes firstly of the British, then the Germans, and also the French family over whose land these battles flow ... so in a way it was an opportunity to explore the universal suffering in that war.

War Horse was spectacularly adapted into a pioneering puppetry stage show in Britain by the National Theatre. It became a resounding critical and commercial success, and was subsequently turned into a blockbuster film of the same name by acclaimed director Steven Spielberg. Even in the twenty-first century, the First World War has lost little of its draw for audiences and artists alike.

REMEMBRANCE ON THE STAGE

The stage has always been a dearly-held part of British culture, and music halls were used in the early stages of the war as a fertile army recruiting ground. In peacetime the tone became very different. Theatres started to ram home the bloody results of the war to their audiences in plays such as *Journey's End*, written by the veteran R C Sheriff in 1927. Sheriff, who had been very badly injured during the conflict, did not poke hard at politics and strategy, preferring to champion ordinary soldiers' camaraderie and courage. But his play did invite audiences to reflect, and to sympathise with the troubled, alcoholic commander who is its anti-hero. Half a century after the First World War ended, theatre director Joan Littlewood's satirical 1960s musical *Oh! What a Lovely War* drew upon jolly popular songs and music hall vaudeville to underpin scenes of farce, futility and tragedy. Appalling battle statistics conveying colossal casualty figures appeared as part of the stage set, as if keeping score in a sporting contest. Field Marshal Sir Douglas Haig, the most senior British commander during the war,

Above left: A photograph from the first London run of R C Sherriff's play *Journey's End,* which began on 21 January 1929. It had first been performed by the Stage Society at the Apollo Theatre for two nights, beginning on 9 December 1928.

Above right: The final page of the original handwritten draft of the play *Journey's End* by R C Sheriff, which is housed within the archives of the Imperial War Museum (*opposite*). The page is signed by its creator, an army veteran; his play captured the intensity of the comradeship that developed amidst trench warfare.

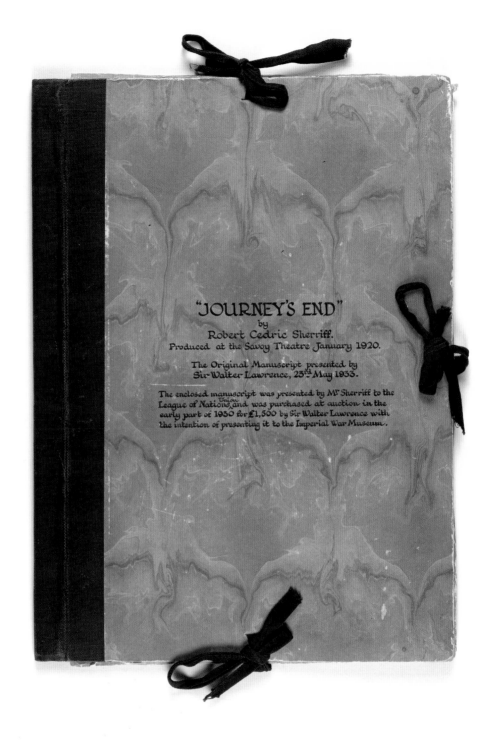

was grimly lampooned as *Oh! What a Lovely War* implied incompetent leaders had betrayed honest, ordinary soldiers. The show was inspired by a 1961 BBC radio programme, *The Long, Long Trail*. The father of its producer, Charles Chilton, had died during the war and his body was never recovered. Chilton's programme fused merry and mordant soldiers' songs with dramatic testimony from veterans who had survived – a compelling

contrast that sparked Littlewood's idea. *Oh! What a Lovely War* hit the stage at a time when appetites for a bold assault on the war's purpose and morality were ripe. Deference to authority was rapidly wilting, and damning historical reappraisals of the war's leadership came thick and fast – namely Alan Clark's 1961 classic book *The Donkeys*.

During the war, people at home had flocked to cinemas to understand what their loved ones were contributing to. Newspapers delivered wordy reports and illustrations gave impressions, but film possessed an unrivalled immediacy. Real scenes of preparations, bombardments, infantry action, the wounded, even the British dead were captured by official cameramen for the 1916 cinema sensation, *The Battle of the Somme*. Captivated audiences experienced the battle for themselves through the 'big screen' while the fighting still raged for real in France.

In peacetime, the cinema became a way of connecting with the First World War. Fictional films told deeply subjective stories about how leaders took the decisions that caused the war and how servicemen and civilians endured, survived or died during it. Generally made with the benefit of hindsight, the most inflammatory films have been accused of rewriting history. The miseries and dangers of trench warfare were imagined in anti-war classics. Retrospective tales stoked empathy with soldiers who were once the enemy and portrayed the war as a senseless calamity. Characters forged by writers, and personified by actors, were an audience's gateway into war – and an immersive commemoration of the human cost.

Over the decades emotive dramas and violent spectacles captivated audiences and generated accolades and awards for their creators. One of the earliest films to be celebrated with an 'Oscar' award was *Wings*, a First World War love story interspersed with elaborate scenes of aerial combat. Made in the silent era of movie making, it starred Hollywood sensation Clara Bow and won the first ever Academy Award for 'Best Picture' at the inaugural ceremony in 1927. A less scathing film version of Joan Littlewood's stage production was released in 1969. *Oh! What a Lovely War* was similarly set to a score of caustic musical numbers in its depiction of the war as a seaside show played out on Brighton's West Pier; its dramatic finale zoomed out from a hillside covered in thousands of soldiers' graves. Cinema has repeatedly returned to the First World War, from *Hell's Angels* (1930), *A Farewell to Arms* (1932), *Dawn Patrol* (1938), *Sergeant York* (1941) and *The African Queen* (1951) through to *Gallipoli* (1981) and a 2018 remake of *Journey's End*.

The invention of the television was a pivotal moment in shaping memory of the First World War, in the form of documentaries, dramas and even comedies. Graphic archival footage and interviews with veterans were broadcast into millions of living rooms in the BBC's 1964 series *The Great War*. The visual impact of the footage engrossed viewers in homes across the country. Two decades later, the searing conclusion to the historical comedy *Blackadder* left behind its standard grim humour and concluded with a moment of tragedy as Captain Blackadder and his men are ordered into battle. Once again, military leaders were depicted as having casually and callously sent their men 'over the top' to their deaths. These television classics, both fiction and factual, became part of the tapestry of informal remembrance in Britain.

Memories of the First World War were also conjured through song. Singing on the march was a widespread soldiering habit, and tunes such as 'It's a Long Way to Tipperary' and 'Pack Up Your Troubles In Your Old Kit Bag, and Smile, Smile, Smile!' were huge wartime hits at home and on the fighting fronts. They remain as recognisable today in evoking the day to day grind of soldiering. Classical music was also a conduit for remembrance.

A poster advertising the first annual Festival of Remembrance at London's Royal Albert Hall in aid of the Haig Fund for veterans in need in November 1919. *A World Requiem*, a new work composed by John Foulds, was billed as a 'Cenotaph in Sound'.

ROYAL ALBERT HALL
Manager - HILTON CARTER, M.V.O.
UNDER THE MOST GRACIOUS PATRONAGE OF
THEIR MAJESTIES THE KING & QUEEN
IN AID OF
FIELD MARSHAL EARL HAIG'S APPEAL FOR
EX-SERVICE MEN OF ALL RANKS (British Legion)
Patron - H.R.H. THE PRINCE OF WALES
AND IN THE PRESENCE OF
Field Marshal EARL HAIG & COUNTESS HAIG
A WORLD REQUIEM
JOHN FOULDS
(CONDUCTED BY THE COMPOSER)
ARMISTICE EVENING
TUESDAY, NOVEMBER 11 at 8
Second Annual Festival Commemoration Performance
FOR ALL WHO FELL IN THE GREAT WAR.
Soloists:
IDA COOPER
OLGA HALEY
FRANK MULLINGS
HERBERT HEYNER
The London Cenotaph Choir of One Thousand Voices.
Boys' Chorus (London Choir School).
The Royal Philharmonic Orchestra.
Tickets (including Tax):
Boxes: Grand Tier, £5 5s. Loggia, £4 4s. Second Tier, £2 12s. 6d. Stalls, 12s. 6d.
Arena, 10s. 6d. Balcony Reserved, 7s. 6d. and 5s. 9d. Gallery Prom., 2s. 4d.
FROM THE BOX OFFICE, ROYAL ALBERT HALL, AND USUAL AGENTS.
Vail & Co., London, E.C.1.

John Foulds' *A World Requiem* was composed as a memorial to the war dead. It was billed as 'a Cenotaph in Sound', such was its epic quality, and premiered at the British Legion Festival of Remembrance in London's Royal Albert Hall on 11 November 1923.

More recently popular bands have written scathing critiques of the war in sympathy with those who were killed during the conflict. 'Butcher's Tale (Western Front 1914)' by The Zombies (1968) told the story of a battle from a soldier's viewpoint. The lyrics in the (incorrectly spelt) 'Paschendale' (2003) by the rock band Iron Maiden described a scene of devastation in which 'lifeless bodies hang on barbed wire'. The album *1916* by Mötorhead was released in 1991. Its title track was a tribute ballad, inspired by frontman Lemmy's interest in the Battle of the Somme, the human cost of which he later referred to as a 'whole generation destroyed'. In 1982 Paul McCartney, one of biggest names in twentieth-century music following the phenomenal success of The Beatles, released a solo effort inspired by the war. The accompanying video to 'Pipes of Peace' recreated the famous Christmas Truce of 1914, when fighting ceased in some quarters on the Western Front and Britons and Germans briefly fraternised. In McCartney's video he plays a British and a German soldier who meet up in no man's land.

A MUSEUM OF WAR

Popular culture and performance did much to refresh – or calcify – attitudes about the First World War, and keep remembrance of it alive, however subjectively. Museums brought another dimension to cultural remembrance. Before the First World War, they were associated with exotic curiosities; objects from far-flung places and cultures dominated showcases. This was to change with the idea of a war museum, established in Britain to create a record, in perpetuity, of the ongoing, world-changing war.

The idea was first conceived during the First World War, after the titanic Battle of the Somme had ended in an indecisive impasse in 1916. The casualties sustained made it all the more important for the British public to be reminded, by whatever means possible, why the war was being fought. Around this time Sir Albert Mond, a Member of Parliament and the First Commissioner of Works, wrote to the Prime Minister, David Lloyd George, with his novel suggestion of a museum.

Battlefields were strewn with man-made matter. Weaponry and officially issued personal kit joined souvenirs made by local civilians behind the lines – hugely popular on the Western Front – in the accumulation of the war's physical evidence. Every object had the potential to unlock a personal or broader perspective of the First World War. Advocates of a new museum for the nation realised that the best opportunity to collect this revealing 'material culture' was before the conflict itself ended. After it was over, objects might be lost in clearance or pass into private hands. Collecting acquisitions from the fighting fronts would be the initial focus of a new war museum's work – if the idea was approved.

The museum's existence and funding were controversial from the outset. The notion was robustly debated in the House of Commons. Captain William Benn MP was weary about the idea of a museum that perpetuated memory of the conflict itself, declaring that 'I have no interest in the Imperial War Museum and I think most people are tired of the whole business'. A heated debate ensued, with Sir Alfred Mond sternly rebutting such fatigued sentiments:

> The hon. and gallant Member opposite, who took a most distinguished part in the War, says he does not want to hear anything more about the War, but we are not dealing with the present time. We are dealing with the hon. and gallant Gentleman's great-grandchildren, who will be intensely interested to see the aeroplane in which their distinguished ancestor flew in the Great War. That is the view which we have taken of the matter and which we must take. It is not an institution for now, it is not a show for the present day, but a great record of a great Empire's greatest sacrifice.

The sternest resistance to the concept came from Joseph Kenworthy MP:

> We should forbid our children to have anything to do with the pomp and glamour and the bestiality of the late War, which has led to the death of millions of men. I refuse to vote a penny of public money to commemorate such suicidal madness of civilisation as that which was shown in the late War.

He was supported by MP Thomas Myers:

> My view is that the general public desire to forget as much as possible the facts of the War. It is quite sufficient for the general public to remember that over 800,000 British soldiers have fallen in the conflict, and that of itself is quite sufficient recollection for the various families in different parts of the country whose members have paid the penalty and rendered their tribute in that direction.

The majority of members, however, supported the idea, even if they treated it with bleak humour. Jack Jones MP declared: 'I shall support the right hon. Gentleman opposite in his desire to have a museum, and I only hope that all those who advocate war will be preserved in glass cases.'

The War Cabinet approved the suggestion of a new museum about the ongoing 'Great War', with the idea formally ratified on 5 March 1917. The Imperial War Museum was formally established by Act of Parliament in 1920. Initially christened as the 'National War Museum', its name was changed to the Imperial War Museum at the request of the India and Dominions Sub-Committee better to reflect the institution's remit to collect material relevant to the efforts of Britain's vast imperial forces during the war. The Board of Trustees included appointees of the governments of India, South Africa, Canada, Australia and New Zealand.

The first Director General of the Imperial War Museum was art historian and mountaineer Sir Martin Conway. Initially he had advocated that the new museum should act as a memorial as well as a museum. Sir Alfred Mond was also keen and raised the matter in Parliament:

> If it became the great Imperial War Memorial, this House and the country might consider it more reasonable to enshrine it in a noble and dignified building than to spend large sums of money in monuments and statues scattered all over the country.

But the proposed memorial purpose was dismissed by the War Cabinet. It was settled that the new institution would be solely a museum, albeit one in need of objects and a home. A frenzy of collecting began. Its sub-committees for the army, navy, munitions production and women's war work all sought to find material that reflected personal experience rather than mere examples of type. The museum's first curator Charles ffoulkes and his team collected objects directly from the fighting fronts. Canadian officer Major Henry Beckles Willson was chief among these early collectors. Such an endeavour was utterly novel in the museum world – to collect objects before the subject of the museum itself was fully concluded and understood. The merits of every item collected, by arrangement with the military or in collaboration with individuals, were robustly justified and corroborated in early documentation procedures:

> If any history of the Exhibit is given connecting it with an Incident, Regiment, Individual or Place, this should be certified in writing by a competent authority, independent of the Collector or Officer in charge of the Section.

The museum did not just rely on its own discoveries. It issued a rallying call for people to send in items of relevance, even with the war's conclusion hugely uncertain. The appeal was lodged within official food ration books and distributed across the country. It asked for:

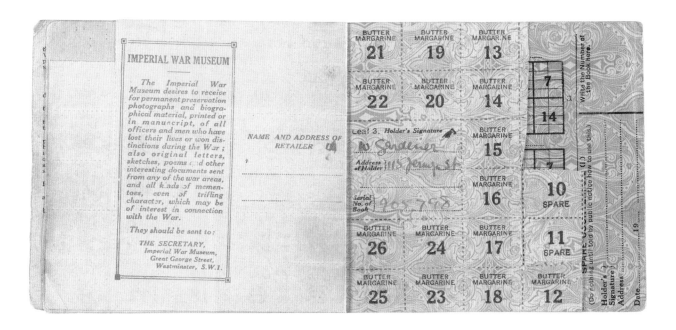

...photographs and biographical material, printed or in manuscript, of all officers and men who have lost their lives or won distinctions during the War; also original letters, sketches, poems and other interesting documents sent from any of the war areas, and all kinds of mementoes, even of trifling character, which may be of interest in connection with the War.

The museum's collections burgeoned rapidly in peacetime. Over the next hundred years they were swollen further by the acquisition of personal and official documents, photographs, film, oral history recordings, books, artworks and equipment. Official papers, intimate diaries, paintings, prints, drawings, sculptures, pioneering battle documentary film and hundreds of thousands of striking photographs all found a home in the collections of the Imperial War Museum. Everything from uniforms, badges, insignia and flags, personal mementoes, souvenirs, 'trench art', medals and decorations, firearms, ammunition, swords and clubs, became precious inclusions. Each item, including the largest weapons of war such as boats and aircraft, told a story about what it was like to live through the First World War. Eventually the museum's collections related to the military services, the vital role played by women during the war, the experiences of children, medical advances, war production and an array of insights into social life during the war years.

In its earliest days the homeless Imperial War Museum connected with the public through temporary exhibitions at a variety of venues. Eventually the Crystal Palace was set upon as an established home.

Its cast-iron and plate-glass structure, set on top of a dramatic natural elevation in south London, had originally re-housed the Great Exhibition of 1851. By the time the museum opened there in July 1920, over 150,000 items had been collected. At the formal opening Sir Alfred Mond, the driving force behind its establishment, declared that 'it was hoped to make the museum so complete that every one who took part in the war, however obscurely, would find therein an example or illustration of the sacrifice he or she made'. He was adamant that the museum 'was not a monument of military glory, but a record of toil and sacrifice'. It was to prove a compelling message, with 4 million people visiting the museum during its first four years.

Dramatic and spacious as the Crystal Palace building was, it soon proved itself entirely unsuitable for the care of collections. The museum moved, reopening in the Imperial Institute in South Kensington on Armistice Day 1924. After a decade, it uprooted again in 1936 to its now-

George V addresses the attendees at the opening ceremony of the Imperial War Museum at the Crystal Palace on 9 June 1920. Within four years, four million visitors had paid a visit to the site.

Army Section – Imperial War Museum

The Army Gallery at the Imperial War Museum, photographed shortly after the museum first opened to the public in 1920 at the Crystal Palace, London. The museum moved to South Kensington in 1924 and then to its permanent home in London's Lambeth Road in 1936.

permanent home in the former Bethlem Royal Hospital for people with mental health problems, also known as 'Bedlam', in Lambeth. The museum itself became a wartime target during the London Blitz of the Second World War. Most of the exhibits survived the repeated attacks on the city, but a seaplane which had endured the Battle of Jutland was shattered when a German bomb smashed through the Naval Gallery in 1941.

Even before this new devastating conflict was over, the Imperial War Museum's terms of reference – like those of the nation's war memorials – had expanded to cover both world wars. They were extended again in 1953 to include all military operations in which Britain or the Commonwealth have been involved since 1914. Since then the Imperial War Museum has developed into a family of five museums recording and showcasing experiences of modern conflict. But its remit remains the exploration of the causes, course and consequences of war and its impact on people's lives.

Along with the opening of new First World War Galleries, the marking of the war's centenary has seen the museum enter into partnerships which harnessed contemporary artistic responses to the war. *Blood Swept Lands and Seas of Red* took over the Tower of London's moat between July and November 2014. The installation consisted of 888,246 ceramic poppies, each representing the life of a British or Empire serviceman lost during the war. The dramatic 'Weeping Window' and the 'Wave' sculptural elements of the design gave the impression of torrents of blood. The work, by artist Paul Cummins and stage designer Tom Piper, was intended to educate, inspire and remind the public about the scale of British and Empire deaths during the First World War. The installation proved a profound success, with an estimated 5 million people visiting the Tower of London to catch a glimpse during its short tenure. Later both 'Wave' and 'Weeping Window' were taken on a tour of the UK. From 2018 they will go on display at Imperial War Museums London and North.

The complex process of removing the Imperial War Museum's collections from the Crystal Palace to new premises adjacent to the Imperial Institute in South Kensington in 1924. The move considerably reduced available display space.

The Imperial War Museum's permanent home at Lambeth Road in London, site of the former Bethlem Royal Hospital for those with mental health problems, or 'Bedlam'. In this photograph, dating from 1937, the famous naval guns have not yet been installed on the lawn.

Popular culture continues profoundly to influence our impressions of the First World War. The historical accuracy and emphases of many works of literature, poetry, film-making and artistry have proven deeply contentious at times, but the emotional hold of stories that stoked compassion or antagonism runs deep. The Imperial War Museum is a place to visit and connect with the 'social lives' of objects that survived the war, and to remember through understanding the experience of what it was like to fight. For many, remembering the First World War by empathising has become as important as formal commemoration, if not more so. Cultural outpourings have proven emotionally compelling, powerfully shaping attitudes towards the conflict that claimed so many lives.

IN FOCUS

OFFICIAL MEMORIAL ART

One of the most striking ways in which the First World War was reflected in culture came in the form of art memorials. These public works of art were produced in Britain in unprecedented numbers during the war and in succeeding years. They reflected not only the enormous numbers of lives lost, but also the many whose bodies had no known grave. Official commissions were potent symbols of the nation's collective grief.

The artists employed by the government to produce national art memorials had a daunting task. In their work, which included paintings as well as sculpture, they were being asked to represent family bereavement and national mourning simultaneously, and to resonate with people across class-riven British society. Artists drew on memorial art traditions of realism and neoclassical styles, while some used modernist imagery.

Official commissions to commemorate the First World War were debated rigorously, especially when artists tried to move beyond the traditional naturalism and religious iconography usually associated with memorial art. Reactions to modernist works in particular were often polarised. In response to two works of memorial art, one critic in 1923 wrote in an article titled 'Artists in Revolt':

Both of these examples, far from being related to the objects for which they were intended, are works of art which challenge and flout public sentiment.

If artists choose to produce such works as illustrative of their own vision and on their own responsibility nobody can quarrel with them; but it seems to me that they are not entitled to thrust their own exceptional views upon work commissioned to interpret public sentiment or public sorrow.

The most famous example of government-commissioned memorial art produced towards the end of the war was *Gassed*, the epic creation of John Singer Sargent (overleaf). His painting depicts young British soldiers, temporarily blinded by poison gas, being led in groups to a medical dressing station. They form lines, hand on shoulder; others lie incapacitated on the ground. This painting's focus upon the suffering and hardships of war is complemented by a note of redemption, as suggested by the football game in the background of the composition. The sport offers a sign of hope, revealing life's continuation in spite of death on such a scale.

When the painting was first displayed to the public, at the Royal Academy in May 1919, the press

---

Opposite: Eric Kennington (1888–1960), Maquette for *The Soissons Memorial to the Missing* (1927), plaster. The architects of the *Soissons Memorial* recommended Kennington as a sculptor to the Imperial War Graves Commission. He had produced an impressive body of work as an official war artist, and had served as a private in The Kensingtons 13th London Regiment.

reported large crowds. The critical response was overwhelmingly positive. Yet the painting's realism had a physical effect upon some people, confronted by the sight of writhing bodies suffering from the effects of a gas attack. Following the display of the work in 1920, it was reported:

> A young girl who was looking at the painting called 'Gassed' by Mr. Sargent, R.A., at the Crystal Palace yesterday, gave a gasp and fainted. When she recovered she explained that her brother had lost his life through being gassed in France, and that the realism had been too much for her.

The public had seen images from the front by way of official art, illustrated magazines and official photography throughout most of the war years. However, scenes of wounded or dead British soldiers had been closely monitored, and often censored, by the government. Many artists believed the only way truly to memorialise the war was to represent the reality of what British soldiers had endured.

Singer Sargent was one among a group of artists commissioned to create a series of memorial paintings. In 1918 the British War Memorials Committee (BWMC) was established within the Ministry of Information. It had the task of commissioning a collection of paintings and

sculpture to serve as a memorial to all Britons who had lost their lives in the First World War. The scheme had high ambitions, with the Committee members hoping that their endeavour would be remembered, not only for commissioning '... the greatest artistic expression of the day, but the practical foresight of those responsible for such a legacy to posterity'.

In order that Singer Sargent should be able to make a picture that was a 'truthful' representation of the war, the BWMC arranged for him to visit the Western Front — something they did for other artists they commissioned as well. Artists visiting the Front had their expenses met and were often given a military commission. This was usually a fairly high rank, enabling them to move around easily without being impeded by army officers. Travelling to the Western Front in July 1918 with fellow artist, Professor Henry Tonks, Singer Sargent made sketches of gassed soldiers he had witnessed. In a letter to a friend he elaborated: 'The Ministry of Information expects an epic — and how can one do an epic without masses of men?'

John Singer Sargent (1856–1925), *Gassed* (1919), oil on canvas. Singer Sargent was approached by the Prime Minister, David Lloyd George, and asked to create a memorial painting. He travelled to France in 1918 and witnessed the aftermath of a poison gas attack on British soldiers, which he decided was a fitting subject.

John Singer Sargent (1856–1925), 'Study for *Gassed*: study of a medical orderly' (1918–19), charcoal on paper. The sketches for Singer Sargent's *Gassed*, including this one, formed the foundation of the large oil painting. In many cases the artist made immediate sketches of the poisoned soldiers as an onlooker.

John Singer Sargent (1856–1925), 'Study for *Gassed*: study of soldiers with bandaged heads' (1918–19), charcoal on paper. This drawing shows three studies of soldiers, their eyes bandaged, lying down to recover from a gas attack. Their heads rest on improvised pillows made from blankets and their personal-issue equipment.

It was intended that the BWMC paintings would reflect the whole of the British war effort, commemorating the work of both men and women and presenting ordinary people in the paintings rather than prominent official figures. The commissioners hoped that the paintings would be arranged in a purpose-built memorial gallery for the public. In a letter written in 1919 Muirhead Bone, Britain's first official war artist and key advisor to the BWMC, outlined his vision for this memorial gallery; he envisaged 'a kind of Pavilion' located centrally in London. The commissioned paintings, including *Gassed*, were to be complemented by sculptural friezes that would convey the nature of the war.

Charles Sargeant Jagger was commissioned by the BWMC to create a bas-relief fragment that would become a model for a large sculptural frieze to sit within the memorial gallery. He was perhaps Britain's best-known memorial sculptor, and a soldier artist. Schooled in the 'new sculpture' tradition, Jagger incorporated harsh realism in his memorial works. He proposed two possible subjects for the fragment, and it was decided that the focus would be 'expressing the horror of war .... and a sort of just retribution'. The fragment became his plaster frieze called *The Battle of Ypres, 1914: The Worcesters at Gheluvelt*.

The Battle of Ypres was unique in Jagger's work because it showed German and British armies in the pitch of battle. Due to its rawness in revealing violence and the moment of death, it was well received when first exhibited at the Royal Academy in 1919. Jagger went on to create many more sculptural war memorials; he characteristically tackled the subject head-on rather than hiding meaning in allegory and symbolism. Jagger claimed that his experiences as a soldier gave him authority to represent the reality of war. Speaking of his war memorials, he declared: 'I got to love the Tommy in the trenches and I've tried to show him as I knew him – not as he looked on parade at home.'

The realism and upfront quality to his work meant that some people regarded Jagger's war memorials as brutal and irreligious. However, his approach was appreciated by many of his commissioners, including the Royal Artillery for his dramatic memorial at Hyde Park. The regiment approved of the 9.2-inch howitzer that adorns the top of the sculpture, even though it made the memorial the object of criticism because of its aggressive imagery. Jagger himself deliberately intended for this monument to remind people of the violence of war. One 'young gunner' was quoted in the *Manchester Guardian* commenting on the Royal Artillery Memorial: 'See that man carrying the shells. He is real. All the green men are real.'

In the early and ambitious days of the BWMC, the commissioned paintings were, as a whole, intended to represent and commemorate all aspects of the war effort. This included the war on land, at sea and in the air, as well as on the home front. George Clausen's *In the Gun Factory at Woolwich Arsenal,1918* depicts a home front scene from a munitions factory. Like *Gassed*, it contained imagery that bordered on religious without being explicit.

Clausen's work was supposed to be paired when hung with a painting by Anna Airy. She was the only female artist to be approached for a commission by the BWMC. Airy was asked to produce a munitions factory scene showing women at work; her contract stipulated a right of refusal on behalf of the commissioners. Although she carried out her commission, her painting was not accepted after being viewed by the Committee. After the refusal, Airy commented in a letter: 'Allright - the 'Munition Girls Leaving Work' came back yesterday and will shortly be found in pieces in the dust-bin.' She was compensated with another commission of munitions paintings, which remain incredibly arresting.

From March 1918 to March 1919, a wide range of British artists from different generations and stylistic schools produced a number of large-scale oil paintings for the BWMC. Many were commissioned from younger modernist artists who had experienced the conflict first-hand. These included the brothers Paul and John Nash, C R W Nevinson and the vorticists Percy Wyndham Lewis and William Roberts. Lewis's *A Battery Shelled* depicts the work of men and machines in the artillery regiments of the Western Front. Developing ideas that he used in earlier vorticist works, such as cubist fragmentation and a natural environment invested with man-made qualities, Lewis showed British soldiers responding to the shelling of their battery. The reaction of the various figures is as fragmented as the churned soil and plumes of smoke – some are portrayed scurrying for cover while a group in the foreground looks on with calm detachment.

A disagreement between the BWMC and the newly established Imperial War Museum partly disrupted the Committee's ongoing work. Sir Alfred Mond, one of the founders of the museum, questioned the purpose of the BWMC. As the Committee was operating within the Ministry of Information, it was technically

George Clausen (1852–1944), *In the Gun Factory at Woolwich Arsenal, 1918* (1918), oil on canvas. Clausen's painting depicted the vast munitions factory at Woolwich Arsenal in south-east London. Aspects of the painting, such as the shafts of light streaming in from the ceiling to illuminate the workers, have an almost religious feel.

Anna Airy (1882–1964), *A Shell Forge at a National Projectile Factory, Hackney Marshes, London, 1918* (1918), oil on canvas. This painting was a particular challenge for Airy, who had to work with great speed to capture the colour of the molten shells. The tremendous heat of the interior added to the intensity; on one occasion the ground became so hot that the artist's shoes were burned off her feet.

supposed to be funding art as propaganda. The memorial element to its commissions arguably did not meet this requirement. This power struggle led to the BWMC coming under scrutiny from the Ministry.

At the end of the war in November 1918 the Committee was dealt a final blow with the closure of the Ministry. It meant that funding for their scheme was not readily available. The newly restructured Committee that included representatives from the Imperial War Museum tried to keep the enterprise going: 'It was thought that the existing Committee should be kept together, though the Ministry of Information ceased to exist.'

However, government funds were desperately needed for rebuilding after the war, and not every cultural enterprise could be supported. A decision was taken by the Treasury to force the closure of the BWMC scheme. In contrast the Imperial War Museum continued, and the Committee's commissioned paintings were transferred to IWM's collection in March 1919. The imagined 'Hall of Remembrance' was never realised.

When the BWMC commissions joined other official war artist work in the IWM collections, before the museum had its own display space, it was decided that an exhibition of war art would be held at the Royal Academy to showcase the material. *The Nation's War Paintings* exhibition was held from December 1919 to February 1920. It ran longer than originally planned as a result of its popularity. Before the show had even opened, it had stirred up controversy. One of the commissioned artists, C R W Nevinson, had tried to display his painting *Harvest of Battle* at an earlier exhibition held at the Royal Academy in May 1919. When the IWM stopped him from putting on this 'preview', Nevinson was quick to sense a press opportunity. He convinced a journalist from the *Daily Express* to report that his painting had been deemed too horribly realistic to be displayed:

> The sensation of the Royal Academy this year will be a picture which will not be there... the Government has refused to allow it to be shown... he has put the dismal soul of the real thing into this picture.

In the end Nevinson's painting was displayed as planned in the December show.

The critical reaction to *The Nation's War Paintings* and the BWMC paintings that were displayed was generally positive, although it did arouse debate about what war art and memorial art should be and how should it look. In particular the appropriateness of spending public money on the modernist BWMC paintings was raised in the House of Commons by Sir Clement Kinloch-Cooke MP:

> Is the right hon. gentleman aware that £9,000 has been spent on these freak pictures, and does he think these freak pictures are a proper representation of the war to give to future generations?

Some members of the public also reacted with disgust. When the exhibition toured to Manchester Art Gallery, one soldier was quoted as saying: 'Their studies of the British Tommy cannot be regarded as particularly flattering. Taken as a whole they look an ill-conditioned, clownish, spiritless lot of men, with some Chaplinesque feet.'

But the canvases painted by the younger artists with personal experience of wartime service, such as the Nash brothers, Stanley Spencer and Henry Lamb,

were regarded by many members of the press as encapsulating a genuine impression of the war. The critic R H Wilenski gave voice to this position when he wrote: 'There are two kinds of pictures in the present exhibition ... the pictures by men who were tortured by the war and the pictures by men who were not.'

The Nation's War Paintings exhibition demonstrated that modernist styles could be eloquently utilised in memorial art; in so doing it set a precedent for further official commissions of this nature. The example was followed by the Imperial War Graves Commission for the second-ever British memorial to be erected on the Western Front, which featured a controversial centrepiece by Eric Kennington, a young modernist artist. The figure group of three 9-foot tall 'Tommies' became known as the 'Soissons Trinity'.

The Soissons Memorial to the Missing in its entirety was created by the architects G H Holt and V O Rees; its sculpted friezes were by Allan Howes and Herbert Hart served as assistant to Kennington on the centrepiece. Located some 60 miles (100 km) north-east of Paris, the memorial site commemorated almost 4,000 men of the British forces who died during the Battles of the Aisne and the Marne in 1918 and who have no known grave.

The Trinity stands imposingly in a line wearing greatcoats, with the two end figures carrying box respirators. At their feet is the common symbol for a battlefield grave: a rifle driven into the soil against which rests a steel helmet. The three 'Tommies' are the solemn and eternal guardians over this site of the dead. Kennington's modernist style favoured blockish solid forms over naturalism. He was inspired by ancient carvings from a variety of cultures, but particularly an Easter Island ancestor figure that he had studied in the British Museum's collection. Kennington described these figures as 'essence of PERMANENCE. TRANQUILLITY – undisturbed and perfectly controlled'. They were a fitting model for the sculpture which he hoped would embody a sense of 'majesty and peace'.

Kennington created the final sculpture in 1928. He arrived at Soissons and carved the monument directly from Euville stone. While the final memorial figures remain true in their form, style and detailing to the maquette (model) held in the Imperial War Museum's collection, there are slight differences in the faces of the Trinity. The stylisation of the figures allows them to be peaceful, monumental and characterful, yet also

Percy Wyndham Lewis (1882–1957), *A Battery Shelled* (1919), oil on canvas. Lewis was a founder member of the vorticist group, a literary and artistic movement that celebrated the machine age. He served as a Battery Officer on the Western Front between May and November 1917, in direct contact with the most modern weaponry of the war.

representative of the many. Kennington aimed for the sculpture to be in harmony with the surrounding memorial, and he even considered the aesthetic appeal of the monument in the distant future, once the details had been eroded naturally over time. Reactions were not all favourable. One writer to the conservative *Morning Post* newspaper complained that the 'Soissons Trinity' resembled 'soulless mechanical puppets, or even worse a group of Aztec tribesmen waiting at the foot of a sacrificial altar'. At the unveiling of the memorial, however, the Mayor of Soissons was impressed by the sculpture, believing it to capture the 'calm and impassive courage' of the British troops he had seen fighting in France.

The artists creating official memorial art were deeply moved by their subject and strove to do justice to the high ideals they served. They included William Orpen, a keen official war artist. Orpen organised his official appointment through his own contacts and spent a long time in France and Belgium from April 1917 to November 1919.

Orpen wanted to become a war artist so that he could take his art in a new direction. Before the war he was an Edwardian society portrait painter, following in the footsteps of John Singer Sargent. The best-known of the official war artists upon his appointment in 1917, he was clearly affected by his experiences during the First World War. In his memoir *An Onlooker in France*, the artist described an encounter with dead bodies behind the lines, and watching young soldiers as they marched towards the front:

> I shall never forget my first sight of the Somme battlefields... Past all the little crosses where their comrades had fallen, nothing daunted, they pressed on towards the Hell that awaited them on the far side of Bapaume.

Orpen achieved success with the art he produced, particularly the reception of his war paintings at the exhibition at Agnew's gallery in London in May

C R W Nevinson (1889–1946), *The Harvest of Battle* (1919), oil on canvas. The work depicts the aftermath of an offensive in the Ypres Salient. Typical of Nevinson's later artistic style, it reveals his determination to show the grim reality of the war.

1918. The Imperial War Museum commissioned him to make portraits at the ongoing Versailles Peace Conference, but when Orpen arrived at the Conference in 1919 he felt searing anger towards the political delegates. On the day of the signing of the Treaty he observed:

> All the frocks did all their tricks to perfection. President Wilson showed his back teeth; Lloyd George waved his Asquithian mane; Clemenceau whirled his grey-gloved hands about like windmills; Lansing drew his pictures and Mr. Balfour slept. It was all over. The frocks had won the war. The frocks had signed the Peace! The Army was forgotten. Some dead and forgotten, others maimed and forgotten, others alive and well – but equally forgotten.

Orpen was determined that the sacrifice of the Allied soldiers should be remembered. He made many portraits while at the conference and created three large commemorative paintings. The first two were group portraits, as per his commission, but he deviated in the third. His painting of a flag-draped coffin was called 'an unknown British soldier in France'. In a letter that Orpen wrote to his long-time mistress, Evelyn St George, he included a sketch of this painting. It showed that the work originally contained portraits of the Allied generals and leaders at the conference, waiting to enter the signing chamber. In the final painting Orpen decided to paint them out.

In a second version of the work he included cherubs floating above and two emaciated, semi-naked soldiers flanking the coffin. Both were based on an earlier portrait of an actual soldier whose clothes had been torn away in a shell explosion witnessed by Orpen. The artist exhibited the painting in this state at the Royal Academy in 1923, accompanied by the title *To the Unknown British Soldier in France*.

Orpen's regard for the common soldier and his emotive symbolism were in harmony with general

William Orpen (1878–1931), *To the Unknown British Soldier in France* (1921–28), oil on canvas. Orpen officially donated his painting to the nascent Imperial War Museum in memory of Earl Haig, whom he described as 'one of the best friends I ever had'. The two men had met in France when Orpen was an official war artist and Haig was Field Marshal.

public opinion at this time. His painting became 'picture of the year' by popular vote, but received criticism from some members of the press, confused by the odd mixture of elements. The Imperial War Museum declined to accept the painting as having fulfilled the commission, a decision widely reported at the time. Yet the painting also had its champions within the press. One journalist wrote:

> For myself, the mere absence of the picture it might have been is welcome... Sir William Orpen has said something that needed saying, and as he has said it to the eye and not to the ear, it may not be readily forgotten.

Years later Orpen approached the museum with an offer to paint out the soldiers and cherubs, and it was accepted into the collection in this amended state.

The expectation placed upon artists commissioned to make official memorial art was that their output would serve the greater public interest. Their work was intended to become a fitting tribute to the war dead – arguably an impossible task, given the British public's very diverse attitudes towards war memorials and their different forms. It was also apparent that most of the official artists could not keep their personal feelings away from the subject of the commission. A century on from their creation, however, this aspect has proved to be a strength. These works of official memorial art retain extraordinary power to move those who come across the works, whether at the Imperial War Museum or on loan to other art galleries. They have become a form of remembrance in themselves.

ALEX WALTON
Curator

AFTERWORD

It remains a struggle to comprehend the extent of the First World War's bloodshed: never before or since have so many British people died in a single conflict. A known place of burial on the fighting fronts was only possible for those whose bodies were recovered; many were killed in bursts of devastating violence that made discovery, collection or identification of their remains impossible. When it was possible to lay individuals to rest, it mostly happened far from home and family. This geographical fracture, formalised by the official decision not to bring bodies home, created a permanent barrier to graveside grief. The lack of a homecoming for so many was the essential precondition to remembrance in the forms we know today.

Out of the logistical quagmire of dealing with battlefield fatalities on such a scale, the receipt of much-dreaded news brought torment and hardship to hundreds of thousands of homes across the British Empire. Official notifications of death sparked a tumult of grief – but were also the prompt for tremendous creative endeavour. Physical separation from the dead meant the absence of normal mourning rituals. The sheer scale of death galvanised an industry of commemoration. Lost lives were remembered through a rich legacy of mantelpiece tributes in family homes and diverse community memorials, as well as grand, state-sponsored architecture and compelling participatory rituals.

Methods of remembering were diverse, their origins often fraught with disagreement. How and why people remembered was never shaped by consensus. Arguments raged over issues of appropriateness, sensitivity, inclusion and cost. Questions of value and legitimacy were constantly raked over. Who should be remembered? Who was forgotten? What say should grieving families have in decisions relating to the remains of their own flesh and blood? Was a more thoughtful tribute to the war dead in fact plentiful provision for the needy living? To what extent should religion permeate formal commemorations – ceremonies or building projects – undertaken on behalf of the nation? To what extent has remembrance been affected by the erosion of the British 'stiff upper lip'?

Acts of remembrance ranged from the deeply personal to the highly formal. They manifested through the everyday trinkets shoved into a soldier's pockets, a profusion of stone memorials on village greens across the country and in the creation of grand monuments and institutions to represent Britain and its Empire. Cultural creations became as important to many people in providing an imagined flavour of what it had been like to live through the war, with its boredoms, privations, excitements, dramas and traumas.

The methods of remembering that were established in the immediate aftermath of the First

World War have rooted themselves in British public life. Symbols such as the poppy and monuments like the Cenotaph became a powerful shorthand for the conflict's human cost. Poems, literature and films helped informally to reinforce the impression, held by some veterans and younger people who had not experienced the war, that it was a futile slaughter. The First World War is now a key part of history lessons in schools; it remains a staple of Imperial War Museums' collections and exhibitions to this day. Learning has become, for many, another way into remembering the war's loss of life.

Remembrance is not a static concept and is unlikely ever to be corralled satisfactorily into a universally agreed definition. The scope of this book has been to illuminate some of the many ways in which it has manifested in relation to the 'war to end all wars' – and how the war's logistical battles in dealing with death were so influential in shaping these expressions in Britain.

Yet the conflict did not eradicate violence as many had hoped. Although the number of British casualties remains unsurpassed, the Second World War brought another round of catastrophic bloodshed. Once again staggering numbers of people across the globe were killed in a world war by lethally improved weapons and new technologies. An average of 27,000 people lost their lives every day between September 1929 and August 1945 as a result of the war. In the latter half of the twentieth and early part of the twenty-first century, Britain and its by-then Commonwealth forces were continuously deployed to smaller-scale conflicts, from Northern Ireland and the Falkland Islands to Iraq and Afghanistan. Fatalities have been far fewer by comparison with the numbers killed between 1914 and 1918 and 1939 to 1945, allowing for recognition of losses on an increasingly personal basis.

However, popular consensus for military involvement in conflicts since the end of the Second World War has never been achieved in the same way as that for the world wars, although empathy with the ordinary soldier remains high. Remembrance from more recent conflicts has focused more heavily on the individual, rather than the action in which his or her life was lost. It became increasingly possible

to bring bodies home for burial, with repatriations involving full honours and due ceremony. Individual tributes have developed very modern manifestations, namely social media memorials.

But traditional methods of remembrance retain their original powers of consolation. The poppy symbol is still embraced by millions of people every year, both civilians and servicemen and women. Its originally intended purpose to help veterans in need continues, raising substantial sums every November to fund the work of the Royal British Legion. The desire to wear the artificial flower as a way of remembering the war dead remains strong. But, as a symbol, the poppy has become more contentious as popular consensus for war – especially more recent conflicts – has become harder to arouse. Their fundraising purpose has become conflated, for some, with a belief that to wear a poppy is to show support for objectionable, state-sanctioned violence.

The First World War continues to linger in hearts and minds. Although it has fallen in and out of interest at times, the 1960s and 1990s were particularly notable periods for a resurgence of concern for the events of 1914 to 1918. There were clear reasons for such spikes of interest. In the 1960s international tensions during the Cold War stoked fear of nuclear annihilation. The 1990s saw yet another reconfiguring of Europe after the break-up of Yugoslavia; conflicts founded on nationalist grounds erupted in the very region in which the First World War itself had begun. History seemed very close to the present, charging remembrance of the 'Great War' with new emotion. Today, one hundred years after the conflict ended – and in another period of turbulence and change – our thoughts turn again to remembering and understanding the First World War.

The shape of remembrance has changed again and again, even as some elements appear sacrosanct. In the years after the fighting stopped at 11am on 11 November 1918, remembrance of the First World War has both evolved and endured. Yet there is no certainty that the aim of remembering the war dead of Britain and its former Empire in perpetuity will be achieved. Whether these losses continue to be commemorated, and in what form, is down to those of us now living in a very different world.

SOURCES

IWM COLLECTIONS

© IWM unless otherwise stated

IWM SOUND ARCHIVE

William Chapman (7309)
Stewart Montagu Cleeve (7310)
William Cowley (8866)
George Craik (4116) BBC
William Davies (564)
Basil Farrer (9552)
Jim Fox (9546)
Reginald Glenn (13082)
Alfred Irwin (211)
George Jameson (7363)
Clifford Lane (7257)
Mary Lees (506)
Michael Morpurgo (33058)
Kitty Morter (4089)
Maisie Nightingale (7488)
Ruby Ord (44)
Harry Smith (45)
Harry Smith (9179)
Gerald Spicer (3156)
Lieutenant E W Stoneham (4237) BBC
Raynor Taylor (1113)
Clara Thompson (13661)
John Wedderburn-Maxwell (9146)
Henry Williams (11265)
Joseph Yarwood (12231)

IWM DOCUMENTS

Private Papers of W M Anderson (Documents 5092)
Anonymous First World War Pilot's Diary (Documents.9238)
Private Papers of Lieutenant H D Bird MC (Documents 1004)
Private Papers of B A and Mrs F M Bowell (Documents 4564)
Private Papers of R H Bryan (Documents.13953),
        © Mr Reginald Bryan
Private Papers of Captain J I Cohen (Documents.3520)
Private Papers of Canon E C Crosse (Documents.4772)
Private Papers of S T Eachus (Documents.11667)
Private Papers of Captain Thomas F Grady (Documents.15000),
        © Michael Currier
Private Papers of Mrs M Harris (Documents 11882)
Private Papers of 2nd Lieutenant R G Ingle (Documents.7087)
Private Papers of Major A C L D Lees (Documents.1068)
Private Papers of Lieutenant A S Lloyd MC (Documents.20535)
Private Papers of W J Martin (Documents.2554)
Private Papers of J McCauley (Documents.6434)
Private Papers of Gunner John W McFeeters (Documents.4221)
Private Papers of A Mudie (Documents.11197)
Private Papers of N Newman (Documents.6326)
Private Papers of E Nicholson (Documents.11852)
Private Papers of Lieutenant L J F Oertling (Documents.24631),
        © Robin Miller
Private Papers of Major P H Pilditch (Documents.6874)
Private Papers of Lieutenant G M Renny (Documents.1374)
Private Papers of Isaac Rosenberg (Documents.19511),
        © Bernard Wynick, nephew of Isaac Rosenberg
Private Papers of Major C J Saunders MC (Documents.2540)
Private Papers of E W Squire (Documents.369)
Private Papers of J D Tomlinson (Documents.217)
Memorial Card for Captain C A Town, First World War
        (Documents.605)
Private Papers of A W Whitehead (Documents.19719)
Private Papers of Signaller Arthur Winstanley (Documents.11518)
Private Papers of Brigadier General L J Wyatt (Documents.14122)
Collection of Mourning Cards including one for victims of the
        Silvertown Explosion, January 1917 (Documents.10686)
Ministry of Food Ration Book Advertising the Imperial War Museum,
        11 November 1918 (Documents.8012)
Museum Archive: EN1/1/REP/003
Museum Archive: EN1/1/TOY/009
Tracing of an Original Manuscript of John McCrae's Poem 'In Flanders
        Fields' (Documents.7852)
*The Unknown Warrior: a symposium of articles on how the Unknown
        Warrior was chosen* (LBY K. 60791)
War Artist Archive: ART/WA1/275
War Artist Archive: ART/WA1/521
War Artist Archive: ART/WA1/522
War Artist Archive: ART/WA1/031/81
War Artist Archive: ART/WA1/046/2

NON IWM DOCUMENTS

Black, J A A 'Neither beasts nor gods but men': constructions of masculinity and the image of the ordinary British solider or 'Tommy' in the First World War art of C.R.W. Nevinson (1889-1946); Eric Henri Kennington (1888-1960) and Charles Sargeant Jagger (1885-1934). Doctoral thesis, University of London, 2003.

Evan Charteris, *John Sargent*, New York, 1927

Sir Arthur Conan Doyle, *The History of Spiritualism*, (vol. II), London, 1926

Sir Philip Gibbs, K B E, 'A Soldier Known Unto God', *Illustrated London News*, London, 20 November 1920

Neil Hanson, *The Unknown Soldier*, London, 2005

Graham Hill *The Silvertown Explosion: London 1917*, UK, 2003

Sir Frederick Kenyon, 'War Graves: How the Cemeteries Abroad Will Be Designed', HMSO, 1918 © Commonwealth War Graves Commission, text courtesy of the Commonwealth War Graves Commission

Sir Oliver Lodge, *Raymond or Life and Death*, New York, 1916

Jenny Macleod '"By Scottish Hands, with Scottish Money, on Scottish Soil": The Scottish National War Memorial and National Identity', *Journal of British Studies*, 2010, Vol. 49, No. 1, 73.

John McCrae, *In Flanders Fields and Other Poems*, Toronto, 2015 ed.

Paul O'Prey (ed.), *First World War Poems from the Front*, London, 2014

Siegfried Sassoon, 'The General' © Siegfried Sassoon by kind permission of the Estate of George Sassoon

Upstone, Robert & Weight, Angela *William Orpen: An Onlooker in France*, London, 2008

Moina Michael, 'We Shall Keep the Faith', 1919, cited in Saunders, Nicholas, *The Poppy: A History of Conflict, Loss, Remembrance, and Redemption*, London, 2013

Kevin O'Higgins, Irish Minister for Justice, 1927, cited in Paul Taylor, *Experiences of Southern Irish Soldiers Returning from the Great War, 1919-39*, Liverpool, 2015, courtesy of the Houses of the Oireachtas

Lord Stamfordham, letter to Dean Ryle, 7 October 1920, Westminster Abbey Muniment 63774 B cited in Richards, A., *The Flag: The Story of Revd David Railton MC and the Tomb of the Unknown Warrior*, Oxford, 2017 © Dean and Chapter of Westminster

R H Wilenski, 'The Nation's War Paintings at Burlington House,' Athenaeum, 19 December 1919, p. 1375. Cited in Hynes, Samuel *A War Imagined: The First World War and English Culture*, London: The Bodley Head, 1990

Birmingham Daily Gazette, 10 September 1920

Extracts from the *Daily Express*, 28 March 1919, 12 November 1920 © Express Syndication

Harry Patch quoted in the *Daily Mail*, 7 August 2009

The Edinburgh Gazette, Issue 29802, 24 October 1916

Evening Post (Wellington, New Zealand), Volume CVIII, Issue 60, 8 September 1924

'Memorial to the Unknown Soldier', *Illustrated London News*, London, November 20, 1920; Issue [4257]

London Evening News, 8 May 1919

Manchester Evening News, 22 March 1920

Manchester Guardian (Manchester, England), 12 November 1919, 9 October 1925

'The Great Day – September 30 1928', *The Mosquito* (No.4), December 1928

Pall Mall Gazette, 26 May 1923

The Times, (London, England), Friday, Nov 12, 1920; pg. 12; Issue 42566, Saturday, Nov 12, 1921; pg. 6; Issue 42876, Monday, Nov 12, 1923; pg. 7; Issue 43496 © The Times / News Licensing

All Quiet on the Western Front, Dir. Lewis Milestone, Universal Pictures, 1930. Film.

Anonymous published letter, *To My Unknown Warrior*, Hodder & Stoughton, 1920

Extracts from the Peace Pledge Union website © Poppy Pledge Union, 2018

Extracts from the Royal British Legion website © The Royal British Legion, 2018

HC Debate 9 April 1919, 24 February 1920, 21 April 1920, 10 June 1920, 1 November 1920, 15 May 1928

HL Debate 9 April 1919

Inscription from the coffin of the Unknown Warrior, © Dean and Chapter of Westminster

IWGC statement December 1918 © Commonwealth War Graves Commission, text courtesy of the Commonwealth War Graves Commission

Letter from Ruth Jervis to IWGC, CWGC /1/1/7/B/42, © Commonwealth War Graves Commission, text courtesy of the Commonwealth War Graves Commission

Scottish National War Memorial website

IMAGE LIST

All images © IWM unless otherwise stated. Every effort has been made to contact all copyright holders. The publishers will be glad to make good in future editions any error or omission brought to their attention.

INTRODUCTION
Q 42481, Q 3362, Q 80135, Q 28762

CHAPTER 1
Q 32526, E(AUS) 921, E(AUS) 825, HU 91107, CO 2533, Q 24781, E(AUS) 2078, Q 5624, Q 115126, SP 813, Q 110611, Q 27633

CHAPTER 2
Q 11578, Documents.1004/B, Documents.5323/A, Q 13390, Q 4492, Documents.20535/C, Q 8354, Q 4475, Documents.2306

CHAPTER 3
Q 23612, Q 23688, Q 10378, Art.IWM ART 6321, NPG x154757, © National Portrait Gallery, London, E(AUS) 4945, Q 71252A, Q 23562, UNI 12250, EQU 3681, EPH 950.1, Art.IWM ART 2884, Q 14339, Q 14386

IN FOCUS: THE UNKNOWN WARRIOR
Q 31514, CO 924, Q 70592, Q 98078, Q 70591, EPH 3232, Q 111468, Q 47636

CHAPTER 4
Q 50412, NPG x123028 © National Portrait Gallery, London, Q 100870, Q 51053, Q 100893, Q 100877, FEQ 270, T41-013_1863476 – Thiepval Memorial, image courtesy of the Commonwealth War Graves Commission, Documents.302

CHAPTER 5
Documents.2554/F, Documents.2554/E, Documents.15774/B, EPH 9795, Documents.15774/C, Documents.15774/A, Documents.2554/K, Documents.2554/D, Documents.2554/J, EPH 5586, HU 82199, Art.IWM PST 12217, Q 67309, EPH 2223, EPH 4139, EPH 499, Documents.24631/C © Estate of Lieutenant L J F Oertling, Q 30456

CHAPTER 6
Q 108454, Art.IWM PST 13620, Hearts FC © McCrae's Battalion Trust Collection, 'Shot at Dawn' Memorial Garden at the National Memorial Arboretum by Oosoom is licensed under CC BY-SA 3.0, FEQ 408,

LBY K.3837, Art.IWM PST 13784, TP/2973, © Trafford Local Studies, Documents.5092/D, Art.IWM ART 323, Art.IWM PST 13211 © YMCA England and Wales, INS 5646, EPH 9462, IWM 2009-09-24, Q 53477, EPH 1880, P08254, 081.2© Tower Hamlets Local History Library and Archives, Art.IWM PST 3284, EPH 2171, Q 30056

IN FOCUS: COMRADESHIP AND REMEMBRANCE
LBY_98_1939_1_A, Documents.7779/A, FLA 5394, HU 86968, HU 86970, HU 86969, HU 86972, Documents.11738/D, Documents.16273/E, WEA 4232, Documents.16273/A

CHAPTER 7
Q 31513, Q 58432, Q 14955, Q 31324, 0504/014 Victory parade, Dublin (1919), image courtesy of RTÉ Archives , NPG x162431 © National Portrait Gallery, London, Art.IWM ART 16377 1, Art.IWM ART 3991 b, Q 31498, Q 69112, Q 81759, BRCXM1, © Design Pics Inc./ Alamy Stock Photo, IWM_LOC_2017_005_0377

CHAPTER 8
Q 90017, EPH 9960, M968.354.1.2x John McCrae, c.1914, Courtesy of Guelph Museums, McCrae House, Documents.7852, EPH 2313, Q 23659, INS 8360, EPH 2284, Q 45814

CHAPTER 9
Q 17028, Q 79045, Q 101780, Documents.123_1_1 © Estate of Isaac Rosenberg, courtesy of the nephew of Isaac Rosenberg, Documents.4999¬/F Displayed with permission of the Curtis Brown Group Ltd, on behalf of the Estate of R C Sherriff, © R C Sherriff, 1929, 2018, Documents.4999¬/E, Documents.4999/C, Q 79545, PHO 152, Art.IWM PST 13753, Documents.8012/A, Q 44819, Q 17030, Q 36932, Q 61182

IN FOCUS: OFFICIAL MEMORIAL ART
Art.IWM ART 5734, Art.IWM ART 1460, Art.IWM ART 16162 6 , Art.IWM ART 16162 8, Art.IWM ART 1984, Art.IWM ART 4032, Art.IWM ART 2747, Art.IWM ART 1921, Art.IWM ART 4438

AFTERWORD
IWM_LOC_2017_005_0561

ACKNOWLEDGEMENTS

This book was written during a busy period for Imperial War Museums. Its release coincides with the 100th anniversary of the war's end – the war during which the museum was founded. Over the past four years, IWM has been at the forefront of commemorations of the 'Great War', leading a global network of partnerships with other institutions to mark the centenary of many pivotal moments during that conflict. This book was written in the final phase of these efforts, and is the result of many efforts that may not be obvious at first-hand.

My immense thanks go to Madeleine James of IWM Publishing, who worked with attentive gusto to keep this publication on track at a frenetic time, with Sara Zo in able support. A debt of gratitude is owed to copy-editor Catherine Bradley who nurtured the manuscript on its journey to this point, helping to corral a nebulous subject into a structured narrative. In a book so richly illustrated as this, the text and images were brought together with seamless style by IWM's senior graphic designer, Stephen Long. Anthony Richards was ever-generous in his thoughtful suggestions of collections to consult while reviewing the manuscript with a historical eye. Many thanks are due to my curatorial colleagues who authored 'In Focus' chapters – Emma Harrold, Alan Wakefield and Alex Walton, who each brought their own specialisms to bear on their respective chapters. Richard Hughes provided valuable recommendations for oral history testimony, while Ian Carter – a regular IWM author – expediently appraised the text along the way.

There was a great deal of interplay between work on this book and the temporary exhibition *Lest We Forget?* at IWM North on which I was lead curator. Claire Wilson, Jess Stoddart, Anna Montgomery, Alex Plant, Liz Campbell, and Joe Stephenson made my work on parallel projects as painless as possible with good humour and team spirit.

Tremendous thanks are due to those who provided support and guidance at large in a way this book would have suffered without. This is extended most especially to Hannah Daley. I am also very grateful to Gill Parry, James Shearring, Terry Charman, Ian Kikuchi, Susanna Dale-Simmonds, Heather Millington, Vanessa Rodnight, Ewan Milligan, Peter Waller, Rhona Baillie, Fiona Dunlop and Gary Moir for their own unique contributions to the development of this publication.

At a particularly intense point of work on *A Century of Remembrance*, the sudden loss of my steadfast grandmother, the indomitable Laura Naughton, proved a very trying moment. It brought home the question of how to cope with a profound loss, however so inflicted. Born in 1919 in the immediate aftermath of the First World War, living always – for a time under the bombs of the Blitz – in London's East End, Laura's life came so close to spanning its own remarkable century. It is to her that this book is dedicated.

Laura Clouting
November 2018